# DAMAGED DNA

## The Secrets of Getting Free From Your Past

*Maureen Anderson*

Winword
publishing house

Phoenix, Arizona

SECOND EDITION

Published by **Winword Publishing, Inc.**
3520 E. Brown Road, Mesa, AZ 85213

ISBN  1-58588-147-3
ISBN 13   978-1-58588-147-5

*Damaged DNA*
*The Secrets of Getting Free From Your Past*

Office number for book orders:

480-985-6156

or visit  **www.winwordpublishing.com**

**Printed in the United States of America**

*Dedication*

Ministry is something that is never done alone. When you see a pastor or an evangelist who is reaching large numbers of people with the truth of the Word of God, there is always a team of people behind the scenes, working, planning and giving of their time and energy to make the ministry operate smoothly and effectively. I have just such a team that has worked with me for a long time. Without them, I would not be able to accomplish a fraction of what I do. This book is dedicated to them as a way of expressing my appreciation for their support, their loyalty and their commitment to seeing the work of ministry move forward.

I dedicate this book to my wonderful team: David Crammer, Faith Miranda, Barb Pruit, Don Enevoldsen. Thank you for your hard work.

# Table of Contents

*Foreword
by Marilyn Hickey*

No one gets the point across better than Maureen Anderson, and in a way that is both informative and enjoyable! *Damaged DNA* explains the life of faith—the faith *every* family needs to turn generational curses into the generational blessing we all desire. Read every word. It will make a *difference* to your household, your loved ones and your future.

Marilyn Hickey

*Damaged DNA*

*Introduction*

When you've been in the ministry as long as we have, you see all kinds of people. There are many who leap into a life of faith and they to flourish from the beginning. There are many others who seem to struggle their whole lives. They want to serve God, but for some reason, they keep running into some obstacle that they can't get past. It might be some habit that recurs over and over. It might be some emotional thing like depression. Sometimes it is a physical affliction or mental disorders. It could be family problems or substance abuse.

Our greatest joy in ministry is to see people do well. We delight in being a part of their lives and watching them grow as they experience the blessings that God has for them. By contrast, we have to greater sorrow than to see people struggle. That is why I care so much about the information in this book.

I have faced things in my past that seemed to hang on no matter what I did. I prayed. I quoted the Word of God. I did all the right things and nothing seemed to work. It was only as the Holy Spirit revealed to me what generational curses were and how they worked that I began to see what the problem was. I want to share with you the things that I learned so that you can be free once and for all of those things that have appeared insurmountable in your life.

Ultimately, conquering generational curses is no different than any other problem we face. It is the blood of Jesus and the cross of Calvary that give us the power to overcome. Our freedom is a part of the salvation that Jesus gives us when we are born again. It is a free gift.

Why is it, then, that some problems seem so difficult to overcome? It is the deception of the enemy, plain and simple. The free gift is there, but Satan tries to keep us from even seeing the areas where he has been able to attach himself to our lives. When we don't see what he is doing, we don't address the problem. We become convinced that the problems we face are just part of life and there's nothing we can do about it. So we plod along, unhappy and resigned to our fate.

I want to give you the tools that you need to bring the light of God's Word into the darkest areas of your life in order to expose what the enemy has done in your family and in you. Once you see where the problem originates, it will be an easy thing to step into the freedom of Jesus. His power is there for you.

There are some simple steps that you can take to understand the plan of God and how to move into your Promised Land. We will start by looking at the things that God told Joshua as he got ready to cross the Jordan River and take the land that God promised to Israel. Embodied in a few verses is a wealth of information. In particular, God spoke seven things that carried Joshua to triumph. Those seven things will bring victory to you as well.

First, God told Joshua to live under the grace of God, not to try to accomplish anything by the Law. The same is true for you. You cannot do it on your own. It is only through Jesus and His death and resurrection that you can find the power to overcome.

Secondly, He told Joshua to arise. Likewise, you must take action.

Third, God told Joshua to be strong and courageous. In the same way, you have no reason to fear. God is there to give you all the strength that you need.

Fourth, God promised to always be with Joshua. He promises the same to you. He will never leave you or forsake you. The love of God for you is greater than any obstacle you could ever encounter.

Fifth, God told Joshua to be obedient. That means that you must learn to listen to the voice of the Holy Spirit and determine to do things God's way, not your own way. God knows better than you, after all. As you learn to trust Him, you will find that your life is happier, more fulfilled and more blessed than you ever dreamed it could be.

Sixth, Joshua was to constantly meditate on and speak the Word of God. The real key to doing things God's way is to never let the Word depart from your mouth.

Finally, God encouraged Joshua not to be discouraged. No matter what you face, Jesus can overcome it. No matter what your past has been, Jesus can restore you to a place of great blessing and victory. No matter what has happened to you or what you have done, the power of the Holy Spirit is more than sufficient to redeem you and your situation.

These things are especially important to know when you are dealing with generational curses. By definition, these are curses that you had nothing to do with. They started in past generations, often many generations ago. You weren't the one who brought them into your family, but you still suffer from the effects of them. Rest in the knowledge that they can stop right now. They do not have to continue into your children's and grandchildren's lives. You can put an end to them.

God has great things in mind for you. It is time that you experienced them. Get ready to move into the Promised Land that God has for you. Get ready to live the abundant life that God always wanted you to have.

# 1
## The Promised Land and the Blessings

All my life, I felt like I was under a curse physically. I never could explain it. It was something I felt inside. No matter what anyone said, I felt it. I understand that we don't walk by feelings, but this was something that I just knew and I couldn't get rid of because the Holy Spirit was witnessing to me that I was under a generational curse.

I battled it for years. The worst manifestation of a physical problem came over a decade ago or more. I had rheumatoid arthritis. God healed me of that, but I still had that sense of living under a physical curse.

One day, I had a blood test done and they told me that they found a rheumatoid virus in my blood but not active. I had been healed of that ten years before, so I prayed and I took hold of God's promise to me. He had already given me a verse to stand on.

*Do you not know that your body is a temple of the Holy Spirit, who is in you, whom you have received from God?* (1 Corinthians 6:19)

For over twenty years, I stood on the Word for energy and strength, and God sustained me through it all, but it seemed that I had to fight the same battle over and over. So I pressed into the Holy Spirit to find how I could break that curse once and for all. I found that I was missing an important ingredient in the process. I needed the Holy Spirit to give me a revelation of where I needed to direct the power of the Word.

So when I finally surrendered this situation to the Holy Spirit and asked what I needed to do to be free, the Holy Spirit said that I needed to add a fast. It was then that I saw the victory. What God showed me was a pattern in my family that had gone on for generations. My forefathers on my father's side never lived long. They died in their sixties.

I remember seeing my grandfather when I was a little girl. He carried his Bible everywhere so he must have known Jesus. When I opened his cupboards, they were filled with vitamins. My grandfather tried everything he knew to overcome this curse. But he died of Parkinson's in his early sixties.

I realized that I was doing many of the same things. I was taking all kinds of vitamins. I always try to eat very healthy. I've claimed God's promises for health. But the curse was still there. What I had felt all my life was true. I don't know what happened in my forefathers, but I needed to get free of it. It was a territory that I needed to take so that I could live for the time that God intended for me to live and accomplish all of the ministry and destiny that He intended for me to accomplish.

In 1 Samuel, we see a problem with the high priest Eli who refused to deal with sin in his family. God said that a generational curse would be over Eli's descendants forever and that they would die young.

> *And you will see an enemy in My dwelling place, despite all the good which God does for Israel. And there shall not be an old man in your house forever.* (1 Samuel 2:32)

Another example of the effects of sin is seen in King Saul. He was God's first choice to be the king of Israel, but his rebellion caused the anointing to be removed from him. It didn't just affect Saul, however. It had an impact on all of his children.

> *And Samuel said to Saul, "You have done foolishly. You have not kept the commandment of the LORD your God, which He commanded you. For now the LORD would have established your kingdom over Israel forever. But now your kingdom shall not continue."* (1 Samuel 13:13-14)

As it turned out, Saul's sons died with him (1 Samuel 31), and the kingdom passed to another family through David.  Saul's sin brought destruction to his descendants.  But it also affected the entire nation of Israel.  For the rest of Saul's life, Israel was afflicted by enemies that they were unable to defeat.  The Philistines and others attacked them.  There was civil war within the tribes of Israel and many thousands of people died.  Sin has far-reaching effects that can go on for generations if it is not dealt with.

I don't know what happened in my background but my forefathers were definitely under a curse, and I was experiencing it in my life.  God began to show me the how tos in this area to beat it.  I went on a fast by the instruction of the Holy Spirit, knowing inside that this was a generational curse.  The fast was the detox to cleanse me from the doubt and unbelief to enter into mustard seed faith.  I had spent years speaking God's Word and seeing myself free, but for this situation, I was missing one element—the fast.

My husband, Tom, and I began praying in the Spirit every day about my health and then the gifts of the Holy Spirit began to operate in this area to show us the problem.  God gave me a vision.  I saw a huge white egg.  I was inside the egg and I felt a dark figure over it.  And by this fast, I was chipping my way out.

I am now completely free of that generational curse.  There is no longer any trace of it in me or any oppression over me about my health. The curse is broken, so I know I will live a long and healthy life. I'm full of strength and energy and totally physically blessed. But there was a process that God led me through step by step that brought me to that freedom that He wanted me to have. I want to share with you the same things that God taught my husband and me over the years so that you can be free of every generational curse that has attached itself to you.

You may find yourself living under a generational curse. You may not

> My forefathers were definitely under a curse, and I was experiencing it in my life.

even know where it came from or why it is attached to you. But a generational curse will keep you from possessing the territory that God has already given you. It will keep you from attaining the Promise in that area. It is a giant that must be driven out.

We are going to look at the book of Joshua. It is a picture of being born again and entering into the Promised Land with Christ Jesus. It is a visual aid that God uses so that we can see what is happening as the Holy Spirit works in us to bring us into the New Covenant. We will learn important lessons as we see the way that God took Joshua step by step into the Promised Land.

The name "Joshua" comes from the same root word as the name "Jesus." That root is *yasha*, the Hebrew word for "salvation." "Joshua" means "salvation" or "Yahweh saves." Joshua is a picture of our salvation.

You probably noticed within a short time after you became born again that it did not make you instantly perfect. The old garbage kept coming up. That is the soul area, and there are some obstacles in the way as you make your journey toward the destiny that God has for you. When you enter into the Promised Land, the land that flows with milk and honey, the land of promises and blessings, there are giants. There are strongholds that get in the way of your enjoyment of the blessings of the land. They are trying to keep you from taking the land.

We are going to learn how to get those giants out of the land so that you can experience the full benefits of salvation. Through the death, burial and resurrection of Christ Jesus, we can step into the very health of God. We can take hold of the Word that the New Covenant says is ours through Christ Jesus and get the curses out of our lives forever so that we can live in the blessings.

Understand, as we begin this study, that you do not need to go looking for the giants. The curses become evident to you, as the Holy Spirit removes the blinders. You need to keep your eyes on Jesus. If you focus on the problems, you become sin conscious. When you spend all your time looking at the junk, then junk is all that you will see. When you are sin conscious, you forfeit the grace of God. You get into trying to figure out what you can do in your own strength to overcome the problem, and you step away from the power of God.

> *Therefore no one will be declared righteous in his sight by observing the law; rather, through the law we become conscious of sin.* (Romans 3:20 NIV)

Instead, your goal should be to become God conscious. You need to see the power of God at work through His Word to set you free and bring you into the Land of Promise. Look for the blessing of God, not the problems of life.

*Damaged DNA*

## 2
## Joshua and the Promised Land

Over the years, I have had many opportunities to pray with people whose problems were primarily the result of generational curses that had attached to them and controlled their lives. There was a woman, for example, who was controlled by a religious spirit. It affected everything that she did.

The Lord gave her a dream one night. She woke up in the middle of the night, and the Holy Spirit began speaking to her about a religious spirit. She spent the next couple of hours praying and interceding. In the process, the Holy Spirit showed her how the religious spirit operated and what it was like.

She went back to bed, but the next day she began to realize that she did all the things that were associated with the religious spirit. She went to her husband and asked, "Do you think I have a religious spirit?"

He said, "Yes, you do."

They went on a fast for a couple of days and she realized that both sides of her family had been very religious. They weren't born again, but they were very religious. As she continued praying,

God showed her a vision of a tree. The top part of it was dead. A religious spirit goes beyond what is the Spirit of God and that's where people get into problems. God completely delivered her from that bondage to religion, and she no longer acted out that behavior in her life.

**Death to the Law**

The book of Joshua begins by telling us the first steps we need to take as we enter the Promised Land. The Promised Land that flows with milk and honey is a picture in the Old Testament of the Kingdom of God in the New Testament, with squatters on our land.

> *After the death of Moses the servant of the* LORD, *it came to pass that the* LORD *spoke to Joshua the son of Nun, Moses' assistant, saying: "Moses My servant is dead."* (Joshua 1:1-2)

When Moses is spoken of in the New Testament, he is associated with the law. John 1:17 says that the law was given through Moses. People came to use his name interchangeably with the word "law." They referred to "Moses" when they quoted what was written in the law. "Moses said" or "It is written in Moses" are common phrases. (Matthew 22:24 is just one example.) Moses is a picture of the law.

The law is about what you can do. Keeping the law is a matter of your efforts—how good you can be, how righteous you can be. But the law also is connected to the curse.

> *For as many as are of the works of the law are under the curse; for it is written, "Cursed is everyone who does not continue in all things which are written in the book of the law, to do them."* (Galatians 3:10)

In other words, if you are living under what you can do, that is, the righteousness of your own works and your own efforts, then you are under a curse. If you don't do absolutely everything in the law, then you are cursed. Break one rule, no matter how small and unimportant it is, and you've broken all of the law. You're under a curse if you don't do it all.

So Moses represents the law and everything that it implies. If we look at his life in the wilderness, we see what happened that prevented him from entering the Promised Land.

It happened in the Wilderness of Zin. There was no water in the place they were camped and the people started complaining. God told Moses to gather the people together and speak to a rock, and He would cause it to yield water (Numbers 20:1-13).

But Moses got angry and, instead of speaking to the rock, he struck it with his staff. Because of that disobedience, Moses was not allowed to enter the Promised Land. Moses is a picture of the law. He is a picture of his own ability.

The Promised Land is a land of grace. It is based on what Jesus has done, not on what you can do. To enter, you have to believe God's Word. You cannot work your way in. Moses was called a friend of God and the Bible tells us that God talked to him face to face, but no matter how righteous a person is, he will never be completely perfect. And Moses failed. If you live under the law, it only takes one failure and you've broken the law. Break one part of it and you've broken it all.

Moses was a picture of the Old Covenant. He shows us that we cannot do it in ourselves. We need a redeemer. We need a Messiah. We need Christ Jesus. We cannot earn it through our own works or our own righteousness.

So the first thing Joshua had to realize before he could enter the Promised Land was that Moses was dead. Joshua had to die to the law. And the same is true for us. We have to die to the law in our own lives. We must rely on God's grace. Grace is God's ability working through us. Paul said it plainly.

*I do not set aside the grace of God; for if righteousness comes through the law then Christ died in vain.* (Galatians 2:21)

If I could be righteous without Christ Jesus, then Christ had no reason to die. I wouldn't need Him. But I can't get into the Promised Land, into the Kingdom of God, into that place of being born again in the family of God,

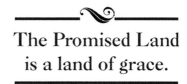

**The Promised Land is a land of grace.**

without Jesus. That means that if I think I can get in by the law, then I'm trusting the law. And if I'm trusting the law, then I'm not trusting in Christ.

In Romans, Paul uses marriage to illustrate this concept of grace versus law.

*For the woman who has a husband is bound by the law to her husband as long as he lives. But if the husband dies, she is released from the law of her husband. So then, if, while her husband lives, she marries another man, she will be called an adulteress; but if her husband dies, she is free from that law, so that she is no adulteress, though she has married another man. Therefore, my brethren, you also have become dead to the law through the body of Christ, that you may be married to another—to Him who was raised from the dead, that we should bear fruit to God. For when we were in the flesh, the sinful passions which were aroused by the law were at work in our members to bear fruit to death.* (Romans 7:2-5)

Put very simply, if you have not died to the
law, you cannot walk with Jesus. It is a spiritual adultery. Living under the law doesn't make
you righteous. Paul tells us that the law actually arouses sinful passions. 1 Corinthians 15:56
says, "the strength of sin is the law." The New
International Version says, "the power of sin is
the law."

We cannot keep the law. If Moses couldn't do
it, we can't do it. We need a redeemer. Fortunately,
we have one. Paul continues in Romans 7 by telling us that we have been set free from the law.

> *But now we have been delivered from*
> *the law, having died to what we were held*
> *by, so that we should serve in the newness of*
> *the Spirit and not in the oldness of the letter.*
> (Romans 7:6)

We are no longer under the law. We are led
by the Spirit of God. We are not under works. We
are under a new law, the law of Grace.

> *For the grace of God that brings salva-*
> *tion has appeared to all men. It teaches*
> *us to say "No" to ungodliness and worldly*
> *passions, and to live self-controlled, up-*
> *right and godly lives in this present age.*
> (Titus 2:11-12 NIV)

Grace teaches. It teaches us to say no to ungodliness and worldly passions and to live a life of self-control and godly righteousness.

The flesh loves the law. We want to be heroes. We want to believe that we can do it ourselves. I experienced this early in my Christian life. After Tom and I were born again, we got into an organization that put us under the law again. We were given many rules to live under. I was to have no shorts, no pants, no mixed bathing, meaning men and women couldn't swim together in the same place, and many other man-made rules.

> The flesh loves the law. We want to be heroes.

I didn't know then that I was to die to the law, and I wanted to get everything right, so I got under the law right away with every bit of energy that I had. I went through the entire New Testament to find everything I wasn't supposed to do. I was so afraid I would miss something.

What happened in those five years that we were under the law was that we experienced the curse of the law. We became poor—extremely poor. We were not poor until we got saved, but living under the curse, we got to the point that we couldn't even own a car. We got sick. We were never sick before we got saved, but under the law, we got very sick. I got depressed. I was a very happy person before I got saved. Under the law, however, I went from a better life to an awful life. After five years of living under the law, I was a mess.

But Paul said it in Romans 7. If I'm born again, then I'm married to Christ. I can't go back under the law. If I'm trying to be married to Christ and married to the law at the same time, then I'm under the curse. We can't be married to both. When we do, we become adulteresses in the Kingdom of God. We need to die to the law so that we can be totally married to Christ.

John 1:17 says that grace came through Jesus. I am now living under grace, not the law. The law has no more control over me.

*For sin shall not be your master, because you are not under law, but under grace.* (Romans 6:14 NIV)

It is vitally important for you to understand this. You need a strong foundation of grace so that you do not become sin conscious. As you get free of generational curses, it is easy to focus on the sin. It is by grace that we are saved and it is by grace that we are set free from the curse. It is by grace, God's ability to work through you, that we get free of all sin.

Trying to live under the law removes us from grace.

*You who are trying to be justified by law*
*have been alienated from Christ; you have*
*fallen away from grace.* (Galatians 5:4 NIV)

If you try to mix grace with law, it isn't grace.
They are mutually exclusive. The law alienates
you from grace. But Jesus already fulfilled the law
through His death, His burial and His resurrection.
He already paid the penalty of the curse in your
life. He paid it in full. You are free from the penalty of the curse. When you enter into grace, you
have received God's power and ability to step into
the performance of the Word that Jesus already did
in your life and now it can become flesh and dwell
in your midst.

That's grace. It is more than unmerited fa-
vor. It is God's very power and ability now that is
working in your life to bring forth the blessings, to
break the curse of your forefathers, to set you free
from the curses of your nationality, to set you free
from inner vows that you made growing up, to set
you free from the dysfunctions of your home and
family, from all the things that are contrary to the
divine nature of God. You get free from that because grace gives you the power to walk out of that
life and into the blessing.

The first step, then, for Joshua to enter the
Promised Land, was to die to the law. Moses was
dead. The same is true for you. As long as you

think you can do it on your own, you will not be able to get out from under the curse. It only happens through grace. We must come into grace. That is where the blessing is.

> *From the fullness of his grace we have all received one blessing after another.* (John 1:16 NIV)

When I step into a life of grace, I receive one blessing after another. That is what God wants for us. The very first thing He did after creating mankind was to bless them (Genesis 1:28)

The word blessed means this. He is giving you the power and the ability, the anointing in your life, to be successful now, to be wealthy, to be prosperous, to be healthy, to be full of joy, to walk in the divine nature of God. That is what God wants for you. That is what living in the Promised Land is all about.

**Arise and Cross**

The time of wandering in the wilderness was nearly over. God's people had spent an entire generation wandering aimlessly. It was time to settle into the Promises of God. So God gave Joshua some specific instructions to prepare him for the conquest of the Promised Land.

*Moses My servant is dead. Now there-*
*fore, arise, go over this Jordan, you and all*
*this people, to the land which I am giving to*
*them—the children of Israel.* (Joshua 1:2)

In this brief statement and the verses following, we can see several steps that we need to take in
our own lives if we want to experience the blessings
of God's promises fulfilled
in us. We have already
looked at the first step.

When I step into
a life of grace,
I receive one blessing
after another.

Die to the law and
embrace grace. That was
the first command to Josh-
ua to prepare him. And it is the first command God
gives us as we prepare to enter our Land of Promise. You cannot do it in your own strength. It is
only by the grace of God.

The second step is that we are to arise. Get
up and get ready. James talks about the balance of
faith and works.

*Thus also faith by itself, if it does not have*
*works, is dead.* (James 2:17)

In simple language, if you have faith, if you
really believe something, you will act on it. You
will arise. Joshua and the people of Israel could
have spent the rest of their lives sitting in front of

Mount Sinai, talking about how great the promises of God were and how wonderful it would be when they got there. But until their faith caused them to arise and get started, the promises were useless.

You must arise as well. You need to settle in your heart that God wants you to go from one blessing to another. That's what the book of Joshua is all about. They were to step into the Land flowing with milk and honey, into the promises of God. We are to do the same. We are to step into what Jesus has done for us in the New Covenant, into what He accomplished on the cross of Calvary. We have to value it and appreciate it enough to obtain it.

The word arise means that I am going to accomplish it now. I'm going to perform what God wants me to do. I'm going to stir it up. I'm going to get up. I'm going to receive the strength, the success, the endurance and the stability that I need to do it. It means I'm going to make a commitment, a decision.

God will never violate your will. He says, "I have this for you." But you have to make the decision that this is what you will do. To arise means to make a decision. I will do this. I choose to take the promises that Jesus bought for me on the cross of Calvary because I believe it is God's will for my life.

Many Christians struggle with figuring out what the will of God is for them. This is a good place to start if you wonder yourself. It is God's will for you to take possession of the promises He has given you. Tom and I realized this about five years after we were saved. And it wasn't just for us. Every promise of God that we took became an inheritance for our children. They have it easy because we fought the good fight. Now we see them just walking in it. We entered the fight. We fought the battle and now they can live in the Land of Promise.

So the first thing is to die to the law so you can enter by grace. Secondly, arise. Take the promises. Believe that God meant everything He said and then act on it.

**Set Your Foot**

The next thing God said to Joshua was a promise.

> *Every place that the sole of your foot will tread upon I have given you, as I said to Moses.* (Joshua 1:3)

God has an interesting way of phrasing things. He said to Joshua, "I have given you the land flowing with milk and honey. I've given you all the promises. Now go take it."

You would think that if God gave us something, then we should already have it. But that is the point so many have trouble understanding.

God gave it to you but it is not yours until you possess it. The NIV says, "every place where you set your foot."

The promise is there but you must bind yourself to it. You must stand on it and determine that you will not move from it. That determined attitude is important because of what happens when you put your foot on a promise. A giant pops up to try to make you move away.

It's kind of like stepping on a tube of toothpaste. You step on the tube and toothpaste flies out all over the place. Step on the promise and out squirts a giant. It's overflowing. It intimidates and threatens you. Everything in you that disagrees with that promise will be squeezed out, and it will attack you. It will threaten you and try to make you feel like you have no faith or your poverty is too great or you are too sick to experience the promise. God gave you the promise but this curse comes against you to block it and keep you from keeping your foot on it.

Remember, though, that you don't have to be strong enough or rich enough or well enough to take the promise. It doesn't depend on your strength. In fact, if you were strong enough and rich enough and well enough, you probably wouldn't need the promise anyway. That's the whole point. It is by the grace of God. That's why you had to die to the law. You can't do it on your own. But God already made provision for that. We draw strength from Jesus.

*I am the vine, you are the branches. He who abides in Me, and I in him, bears much fruit; for without Me you can do nothing... If you abide in Me, and My words abide in you, you will ask what you desire, and it shall be done for you.* (John 15:5, 7)

Until I put my foot on the Word of God, on His promise, I can't do anything. But when I abide in His Word and His Word abides in me, I can ask whatever I desire and it will be done.

God said the same thing to Joshua. "Every place you put your foot, that is your land. That is what God has given you. But you must put your foot on it first."

You need to find the promises that God wants you to live in and get your foot there. You are making a commitment and you're not going to move your foot from that promise until it becomes flesh and dwells among you.

> Step on the promise and out squirts a giant.

The process of possessing your Promised Land, then, has to follow these steps. You have to die to the law and embrace grace in your life. Secondly, you have to make a commitment to arise. Determine that you are done with a life of poverty and sickness and depression. Declare, "I am not going to live like this anymore. God has a better life for me. Jesus already bought it for me, so I'm going to arise."

Next, set your foot on the promise. Bind yourself to it and decide that you are not moving your foot until it becomes a reality in your life. You will not let go no matter what shows its ugly face. Regardless of the circumstances or the situations that confront you, you will not give up.

*May the Lord direct your hearts into God's love and Christ's perseverance.* (2 Thessalonians 3:5)

There will be giants who tell you that you are a failure and a loser, that you don't deserve it. But they are not the end of the story. In God you will find victory. But you have to stand with strength and courage. Because you are in Christ, no giant can stop you.

## 3
## *Be Strong and of Good Courage*

When we began to construct the building that Living Word Bible Church is in now, we had a clear direction and promise from God. We set our feet on that promise and began to build. But of course, there were giants. City authorities came against us. Neighbors came against us. People told us it couldn't happen. Some threatened to take us to court. All around us were voices saying that it couldn't be done.

If we had tried to build it on our own, it would have been a disaster. But the voices didn't matter. The only voice we chose to listen to was God. And He said that when we put our foot on the promise, nothing could stop us because He was there to help. The giants were driven out by God's power.

God reminded Joshua of past victories. He made it very clear that Joshua was not fighting the battle on his own. He had plenty of help.

> *No man shall be able to stand before you all the days of your life; as I was with Moses, so I will be with you. I will not leave you nor forsake you.* (Joshua 1:5)

David was anointed as king. It was the call of God on his life. He had a promise from God. But a giant stood in the way. Saul was already king. And Saul wanted to kill David. He was determined to end David's destiny before it even got started. He committed an entire army to the task. Saul and an army stood against little David.

But could David be stopped? No. God had made a promise and as long as David stood on that promise, God insured that it would come to pass. When God gives you a promise, no one can stop it but you. If you stand without moving from that promise, you will succeed. Stand with courage in the face of the giant and don't move.

So God gave Joshua a fourth point of instruction for taking the Land of Promise.

*Be strong and of good courage.* (Joshua 1:6)

God says the same thing to you. He has given the land to you. What is the land? It is the blessings of God. It is the promises He has made to you in His Word. You can stand courageously and be strong because you do it by God's strength, not your own. God has given you His strength. He has given you the resurrection power of Jesus.

With that power in you, you are a winner. You are already successful. You are on top. You are the head. Nothing can prevent you from taking the Land of Promise.  No giant is strong enough to stand up to the power of God in you.

It is time to get over the victim mentality that has made you so weak for so long.  You must have courage to stand on the promise.  Say goodbye to the victim.  That cannot be a part of your identity any longer.  No more weak little wimp, beaten up and praying for someone to take care of you and make you feel better.  You have to be strong and of good courage.  This is a command from God.

> You have to be strong and of good courage.  This is a command from God.

This kind of attitude is exactly what Jesus had in mind when He said that the Kingdom of God is taken by force.

> *And from the days of John the Baptist until now the kingdom of heaven suffers violence, and the violent take it by force.* (Matthew 11:12)

Some translations say that it is taken by "violence."  It means taking on God's love and Christ's perseverance.  It is the attitude that says, "I don't care what comes against me.  I'm not letting go.  I'm not quitting.  You can drag me through the mud, but I will not move from this promise.  I am strong and courageous."

We can be this strong because the Holy Spirit in us makes us strong. He is there to help us. Paul said it this way.

> *Likewise the Spirit also helps in our weaknesses. For we do not know what we should pray for as we ought, but the Spirit Himself makes intercession for us with groanings which cannot be uttered.* (Romans 8:26)

How does the Holy Spirit help us? The Greek word that is translated "helps" in that verse gives us an explanation. It is the word *sunantilambonomai*. It is a compound of three different Greek words. The Holy Spirit had to create His own word to describe Himself.

The first is *sun* (pronounced soon). *Sun* means "together with." This means that the Holy Spirit partners with us. So I'm not left to face the giants alone. He is right there together with me.

The second word is *anti*. *Anti* means the same thing in Greek as it does in English. It means "against." The Holy Spirit is against anything that opposes us in the possession of our promises. He gets angry and violent like a mother bear who is separated from her cubs. He fights with us against our enemy.

The third word is *lambano*. It means "to take hold of." The Holy Spirit, then, takes hold of the

promise with us. He is there to take back everything the devil has ever stolen from us.

Taken together, those three words mean lit-
erally "to take hold of together with against." *Sunantilambonomai* means that the Holy Spirit partners with us to stand against anything that opposes
us and thereby to take hold together with us of the
promise that we have put our foot on. It means that
we have at our disposal the gifts of the Spirit and the
fruit of the Spirit. We have the same power of the
Spirit that raised Jesus from the dead. How can we
not be strong and of good courage?

The Holy Spirit is there and we have the gifts
of the Spirit available to us. We have the word of
knowledge to show us where the giants are and the
word of wisdom to show us how to deal with them.
The Holy Spirit partners with us to provide everything we need to defeat any enemy that stands in the
way of the promises of God.

## Be Obedient

One thing should be obvious, but for some
reason we often miss it. If we can't take the Promised Land in our own strength but we need the Holy
Spirit to guide us and to empower us, then logically,
we also need to do what He tells us when He tells us
to do it. We can't ignore Him. The fifth instruction
God gave to Joshua was to obey.

*Only be strong and courageous, that you may observe to do according to all the law which Moses My servant commanded you, do not turn from it to the right hand or to the left, that you may prosper wherever you go.* (Joshua 1:7)

You have to obey the voice of God. Be obedient. The Bible says that if we love Him, we will obey Him (John 14:15). When the Holy Spirit shows me things, I will follow Him. If I love Him, I will do what He says and I will win in that area of my life.

But I need to be quick. I need to obey His voice. Jesus said that His sheep hear His voice and they respond (John 10:27). That is my prayer every day. "Father God, I want to hear your voice. I want to be quick to obey. I hear the voice of my shepherd and I obey His voice. Please, don't let me go left or right. If I do, you said that I will hear a voice behind me saying, 'No, no, this is the way. Walk ye in it.' I trust you, God, that You will do that."

As I said earlier, don't go looking for garbage. The Holy Spirit will show it to you when it's time to deal with it. If He doesn't show you something that you need to do, then don't go looking for something. That's where people get into trouble.

You have to trust God. He's the leader. Joshua led the people right into the land where all the giants were, but they didn't just go where they felt like going. They went where God told them to go. They were obedient. And as long as they were obedient, they had success.

God told them exactly how to take Jericho and they did it. But then they set off to capture the little town of Ai. They didn't wait for God's direction. They just did it. And the result was that they were beaten—badly. After that they obeyed.

The fifth step to taking the Promised Land, then, is to learn obedience. We have to die to the law and embrace grace. We have to arise and make a commitment to taking the promises. We have to put our feet on the promises and determine not to be moved from that place until they become reality. We can no longer be victims but we must be strong and courageous in the face of any giants we meet. And then, we must be obedient to the Holy Spirit.

> If He doesn't show you something that you need to do, then don't go looking for something.

### Keep the Word in Your Mouth

The sixth thing that God told Joshua related to how he could consistently obey the Holy Spirit. We've all run into the problem of wanting to obey God but finding ourselves not doing what He tells us to anyway, no matter how much we really wanted to. The key to obedience is in the Word of God. And that is what God told Joshua.

*This Book of the Law shall not depart from your mouth, but you shall meditate in it day and night, that you may observe to do according to all that is written in it. For then you will make your way prosperous, and then you will have good success.* (Joshua 1:8)

The Word needs to be in your heart and in your mouth constantly. You can't speak the curse and expect to succeed. You can't talk the devil's talk. You can't speak victim talk. It has to be the Word of God coming out of your mouth.

This means you will have to change your confession. When I put my foot on the promise, I declare what God says, and I'm not going to change my confession, no matter what.

This is of the greatest importance. It is vital. You won't ever obtain what God has for you if you are double-minded, if you say one thing today and something else tomorrow. You have to get control of your tongue.

*Death and life are in the power of the tongue,*
*And those who love it will eat its fruit.*
(Proverbs 18:21)

You need to believe that your words are full of power and you want it to be the power of God and His Word, not the power of the devil. I am going to keep my mouth on His Word because I love His Word and I will enjoy eating the fruit of what it produces in my life. But to do that, I need to say the same thing God says.

Hebrews says that Jesus is our high priest who has been through everything that we will ever have to face and He overcame all of it. We have only to hold onto our confession.

> *Seeing then that we have a great High Priest who has passed through the heavens, Jesus the Son of God, let us hold fast our confession.* (Hebrews 4:14)

Holding fast means to say the same thing as God. No matter what happens in your life, you are going to let nothing come out of your mouth but the Word of God.

God told the Israelites as they were coming out of Egypt, "Open your mouth and I will fill it" (Deuteronomy 30:14). He told them that He would put extraordinary things in their mouths, things full of blessings, outstanding things that they had hoped and dreamed about.

But they would not open their mouths so that God could fill them. All they did was look at their situation and murmur and complain. They never had the abundant life that God wanted to give them.

It is important that we not become like Israel. God wants you to open your mouth so that He can fill it with extraordinary things, with signs and wonders and all kinds of wonderful things. But you've got to open your mouth. Psalm 103 tells us not to forget all the benefits of God and one of those benefits is that He fills our mouths.

> *Who satisfies your mouth with good things,*
> *So that your youth is renewed like the eagle's.*
> (Psalm 103:5)

God does not want your body to be wasting away. He wants you to look outstanding when you're a hundred years old. It is His desire that everything in your body be operating at full efficiency. The renewing of your youth is a result of having your mouth filled with the good things of God. Learn to do this and you will be filled with the intellect and intelligence of God, with His brilliance. You are made in His image. It starts with your mouth.

## THE POWER OF LIFE AND DEATH

There is power in your tongue. According to Proverbs, it is enough power to bring you life or take it away.

*Death and life are in the power of the tongue,*
*And those who love it will eat its fruit.*
(Proverbs 18:21)

Fruit doesn't just appear in your life. It comes from a seed. The seed is planted and it grows up into a plant or a tree and then one day, buds appear and in time they fall off and fruit grows.

> The renewing of your youth is a result of having your mouth filled with the good things of God.

When we talk about eating the fruit of your mouth, it has the same kind of process behind it. You eat the fruit of what you say. The words that come out of your mouth are a seed that sprouts up, grows and eventually bears fruit. The words you speak are seeds planted for your future. If your words are destructive, then that is the seed that is planted and the fruit will be destruction. If your words are full of death, they will produce death. If all you talk about is your bad circumstances, then your words will bear fruit in even worse circumstances. You become like the murmuring Israelites, planting seeds that have the power to produce what you say.

You have to stop saying negative things. You have to put a stop to every word that is destructive. Be careful of the words that you speak out of habit. People often say things like, "That tickled me to death," or "That just kills me." Don't even let words spoken in jest become seeds that rob you of life. Let God fill your mouth with good confession instead. Do not let the Word of God depart from your mouth.

### Hold Fast Your Confession

Early in our ministry, at a time when Tom had just become a youth pastor, I had a bout with depression. I'm a naturally happy person and I enjoy life. But one day I just woke up in severe depression. It was like I stepped into a place of utter darkness, and I felt no life in me.

This went on for a month. Every day Tom asked me how I was, hoping it was better. And every day I answered, "I'm so depressed. I don't know why. I can't come out of this." I kept asking myself, "Why am I here? How can I get out of this? Somebody help me." Every morning I hoped the depression would be gone, but it clung to me and wouldn't leave. I was young in the Lord and I didn't know what was going on. I just knew I was in a terrible state and I couldn't help myself.

But one day, I made a commitment to change my confession. I said, "Today I'm going to declare that this is the best day of my life. I'm going to talk about it all day long. I'm going to say that this is a wonderful day and that I'm blessed."

I called a girlfriend and invited her to lunch. She asked me how I was and I said, "Blessed, blessed, blessed."

Everything inside of me was screaming the opposite. "You're not blessed. You're in depression. You need help. You need to ask her for help."

But I refused to listen to that voice. I kept saying, "I'm wonderful. It's a wonderful day and I'm blessed." The darkness was still there and it didn't let up. But I kept forcing myself to think wonderful, beautiful, exciting things.

Tom came home from work and asked how I was. "This is the best day of my life. I'm wonderful."

He looked at me like he wasn't sure if I really was okay or if this was an attempt at good confession. But he was supportive and we were both ready to get rid of that depression so he didn't push it.

That night I was studying the Word in preparation for a class that I was teaching. As I sat there, all of a sudden, the presence of God came on me and the power of God hit me and that depression was broken. It was gone from my life. The power of confession worked. For a month, nothing else had made any difference. It didn't matter what I did until I decided that I wasn't going to agree with it anymore.

Confession means to say the same thing that God says. We are now citizens of the Kingdom of God. We want to live in the promises of God. But the Kingdom has certain rules that we have to live by. And one of them is that we have to speak what God speaks. We have to keep that confession in our mouths. That is how Hebrews says it.

With Jesus as our high priest, every problem or circumstance that we run into has been taken care of. He is there to plead our case for us. He died to set us free from the curse. He completed His project. He defeated the enemy, destroyed the works of the devil, and now He is in heaven.

But for Him to do that, we have to come into agreement with what He says. This means that we have to find out what He says in His Word and fill our mouths with it. We must hold fast to our confessions. "Hold fast" means that you will hang on to it no matter what life tries to do to you. No matter how hard circumstances try to pull that confession away from you, you will not let go. Let us hold fast. Keep saying what God says, not what you see.

We are told again in Hebrews not to let go.

*Let us hold fast the confession of our hope without wavering, for He who promised is faithful.* (Hebrews 10:23)

We are to be like flint—solid, unchanging, without wavering or moving. We do not let go of our confession no matter what. This is what it means to stand in faith. We are to be like God. The Bible tells us that God created the world by faith.

> *By faith we understand that the worlds were framed by the word of God, so that the things which are seen were not made of things which are visible.* (Hebrews 11:3)

So we are to be like God. The worlds were framed by the Word of God. He created by His own words. So we create our world by the words that we speak. Words are building blocks. As I keep saying something, I am building something. I am creating with my words. And my words bring into creation whatever I am saying. If I don't see the promise of

> We have to find out what He says in His Word and fill our mouths with it.

God fulfilled in my life, it is because I have not used His Word as my building blocks. I have not said the same thing as God. Instead I have spoken my own words and the world that was created as a result is not where God wants me to be.

If I learn to confess God's Word, then the world that is created by my confession is filled with His life and His blessing. It is created out of that which was invisible. Paul said in Corinthians that we are not to look at our circumstances.  We are to confess what God says, not what we see.

> *While we do not look at the things which are seen, but at the things which are not seen. For the things which are seen are temporary, but the things which are not seen are eternal.*
> (2 Corinthians 4:18)

That which I can see is only temporary.  It is subject to change.  To operate in the Kingdom of God principle, I need to be like God and operate the way He operates.  I have to look at what I don't see because that is eternal.  By making my confession the same as what God says, I'm creating eternity in my life.

God says that in the Promised Land, no matter what you are feeling, no matter what emotions you are experiencing, you have to make a decision that you are going to hold on to your confession and you're not going to let go because your confession has the power to destroy the problem.

## Meditation

God told Joshua not to let the Word depart from his mouth.  He was to develop a good confession, but then He added that Joshua was to meditate on it day and night (Joshua 1:8).  He needed to meditate on what God said, on the promises, so that he could observe to do according to all that is written in the Word of God.

When you meditate on the things that God says, then you begin to obey God's Word because you're not under the law anymore. You're under the power that comes from thinking God's thoughts and letting those thoughts become you. The Bible says that as a man thinks in his heart, so is he (Proverbs 28:7). So you need to meditate on God's words so that they are what you think.

The word "meditate" means "to mutter, to talk aloud, to talk under your breath, to imagine." Once you do those things to come into total agreement with God in your life, then you're going to see the success that God wants to have happen in your life. Then you're going to obey God.

Before, when I got born again in a legalistic church, I went through the Bible and wrote down all the things I wasn't supposed to do because I didn't want to sin against God. But I couldn't keep the law. If I broke one little part of it, I was guilty of breaking it all.

But when I got into grace, I began to think like God and meditate on God and then His thoughts were produced in me and then I could obey Him. I could do the Word of God because it is no longer up to me. It is now the Word of God in me that has changed me so that I can do it.

# 4
## Transformed

Our oldest son Scot always seemed to be under a curse of some kind. As a family, we were blessed, but things just happened to him. Things that should not have been a big deal, when they happened to him, could be disasters.

One time he got hit in the eye with a ball. I was raised with four brothers so I knew that boys get hit in the eye all the time. But with Scot, he almost lost his eye.

Once he fell off his bike. Boys fall off their bikes all the time and they walk away with a few scrapes and bruises. For Scot, his arm was almost paralyzed. Even when he was in his twenties, he had a bad situation occur that was devastating.

God kept coming through every time we sought Him and things always worked out, but it seemed that there was one thing after another. No matter what he touched, it seemed to go bad for him. We asked God to show us what the problem was.

Once we cried out to God, He gave me a picture right away. I remembered a situation when Jason was about three years old and Scot was about five and a half. We were in Vacation Bible School, and at the end, the pastor invited moms to bring their children forward to be dedicated to the Lord. The principle of dedicating children can be traced back to a time before the giving of the law. It is an important biblical concept.

> *Consecrate to Me all the firstborn, whatever opens the womb among the children of Israel, both of man and beast; it is Mine.* (Exodus 13:2)

Even Jesus had been dedicated after He was born (Luke 2:21). I had Jason with me but Scot was still downstairs. So I took Jason up for the dedication. I had never done that with either of my sons. The Holy Spirit said to me, "Go get Scot and dedicate him, too." But I dismissed it. I thought, they're both fine. I'm taking Jason up. They're both born again so everything is good.

The Lord brought that incident back to me. There are many verses in scripture that talk about the importance of dedicating children, especially the firstborn. We had never done that with Scot. I didn't think it was important. Jason had been there but not Scot.

We took care of that problem right away, even though Scot was in his twenties. We brought a financial offering and dedicated Scot right away. From that moment on, Scot's life was transformed.

It completely changed. He now goes from blessing to blessing. He has a wonderful wife and children. A transformation had to take place from the curse to dedication.

### The Process of Transformation

Transformation in our lives doesn't just happen. There are steps that we have to take first so that the Holy Spirit can bring change. Romans gives us a description of how it is that we can be transformed. It requires renewing our minds.

> *And do not be conformed to this world, but be transformed by the renewing of your mind, that you may prove what is that good and acceptable and perfect will of God.* (Romans 12:2)

You are obligated to undergo complete change. Scripture commands you to be transformed. You are responsible before Almighty God to completely change in your life. To do that, you have to renew your mind. That means that you have to think in a new way. It means that you will have new ideas, new plans, new thoughts, and new ways—all by the Holy Spirit.

The Greek word that is translated "transformed" is *metamorphoo*, from which we get the English word metamorphosis. It is the same word that describes the change in a caterpillar. It spins a cocoon and goes in a caterpillar but comes out as a beautiful butterfly, totally changed. It has undergone a metamorphosis. The butterfly and the caterpillar don't look anything like each other. They don't eat the same things. They don't do the same things.

That is the kind of metamorphosis that God puts you through. When you are born again, you become responsible for changing from a caterpillar into a butterfly. That is done by renewing your mind, and renewing your mind is accomplished by meditating on the Word of God.

When you start to think God's way, then you will be ready to operate in the Promised Land. Then you can drive out those giants because you will know the good and acceptable and perfect will of God in your life.

You can plan your thoughts for the day. What does God say to meditate on? He tells us to meditate on His signs and wonders. Meditate on His works. Meditate on His promises. Meditate on His loving-kindness. It is your responsibility to take control of your mind, to bring it into obedience to Christ. You are to take every thought captive. Philippians tells you what to meditate on.

> *Finally, brethren, whatever things are true, whatever things are noble, whatever things are just, whatever things are pure,*

*whatever things are lovely, whatever things are of good report, if there is any virtue and if there is anything praiseworthy—meditate on these things.* (Philippians 4:8)

Remember that the spies came back from the Promised Land and reported what they saw. But God said it was a bad report.

Speaking what you see, if it is not in agreement with God's Word, is a bad report. We need to speak what God says, and we need to think on the good report. Dwell

> Renewing your mind is accomplished by meditating on the Word of God.

on those things that are truth, that have virtue, anything of excellence. You are to give your mind to those things. Make your mind work for you to build your land that God has promised you.

Talk God talk. If you think God thoughts, you are promised to have success and prosperity in your life.

### Discouragement

Tom and I had to overcome discouragement in our lives. At one point, he was a youth pastor. We were building that group with all of our energies. Our whole hearts were in it. We were praying and fasting, and we wanted to be everything that God wanted us to be.

But every Wednesday, which was the evening that we met with the youth, we were flooded with discouragement. We could almost expect it. We'd wake up on Wednesday and we felt discouragement and defeat. We felt that what we wanted in our ministry wasn't going to happen. God loves somebody else better than us. Discouragement tells you that you're a loser and that you're never going to be successful. You can pray, you can fast, you can do whatever you want, but it's not going to happen for you.

But we knew what the Word said and so we battled that discouragement every week. We said, "No, in the name of Jesus," and refused to give it a place in our lives. And one day it broke.

I could tell it was a generational curse because it violated our will. It wasn't what we wanted. It wasn't what I wanted to think or what I wanted to speak but it had power over me. When it's a generational curse, your will is captured and even though you don't want to do it, you don't want to feel that way, you don't want to speak that way, you still do.

We were first generation Christians fulfilling our destiny and the enemy didn't want us to succeed. He didn't want us to become pastors and one day build a church. He wanted us to quit, to give up and to leave the ministry. If we had not conquered discouragement then, we wouldn't be where we are today. But we did conquer it and discouragement is no longer a part of our lives. God commanded us not to be discouraged. I am not going to disobey God. I had to get free of it.

### Be Strong and of Good Courage

God told Joshua to be strong and of good courage. But that meant also obeying an obvious corollary and that command forms a seventh instruction that God gave to Joshua.

> *Have I not commanded you? Be strong and of good courage, do not be afraid, nor be dismayed, for the LORD your God is with you wherever you go.* (Joshua 1:9)

The word dismayed means that you cannot be discouraged. You have to give it up. You can't have discouragement in your life and be successful in the Kingdom of God. It will prevent you from obtaining what God has for you.

Discouragement will drain you of your energy. It will take the strength out of you. It will take the courage out of you. It will invade your mind. It will invade your speech and it will ultimately cause you to quit, to give up and to let go of what you're supposed to be holding fast to. You'll step off that promise. You'll let it go. You'll say that it's too hard because you've allowed discouragement to be the god of your life instead of God being the god of your life.

What happens when you get discouraged? You are flooded with negative thoughts. You start speaking the discouragement. You overflow with words of defeat. You go into depression. You go to bed. You put the cover over your head. You lose all your strength, all your courage. You become a loser. You are defeated and fainthearted. Discouragement is a poison in your life and you have to give it up.

The Bible tells us not to be afraid. We can't have fear, not even a little bit of it. It will cause you to be defeated. If you have fear in your life, you cannot operate in perfect love. God has not given us a spirit of fear but of power, love and a sound mind (2 Timothy 1:7).

Fear is a terrible thing. For some people, it comes on them and they can't get rid of it. There was someone that I knew who had such a strong phobia that she could not even leave her home. She was afraid of all kinds of things.

As we sat and talked one day, she shared with me that she came from a family that was driven by fear. We realized that it was a generational curse from things that had gone on in the family. We began to pray and ask God to forgive her forefathers, and we saw that curse of fear nailed to the cross.

She was totally delivered from those fears. She is now able to leave her home without being afraid and she can now live a normal life, moving in crowds of people without any phobia.

That word "fear" means to dread something that God told you to do. You need to get rid of that if you're dreading something. Anything that harasses you or makes you feel afraid, fearful or terrified is opposed to God's will in your life.

Our youngest son, Jason, was very clingy when he was young. He always seemed to have a lot of fear so he never got far from us. He had always been that way so we just assumed that was how his personality was. We didn't think it was anything abnormal.

> Anything that harasses you or makes you feel afraid, fearful or terrified is opposed to God's will in your life.

But when Jason was eight or nine years old, we were playing a game one day and as we were talking, he began to share some of his fears with me. As he did, I realized that what he felt was not normal. No fear is normal but this was far more than I had realized.

As soon as Tom came home, I shared the conversation with him, and we immediately began to pray. We asked God what was happening in Jason, and we let the gifts of the Holy Spirit start to flow. And God revealed the source to us.

The Holy Spirit showed us that it came in at birth. Jason almost died when he was born. He came out purple and it was a miracle that he lived. He did live but a spirit of death came on him and followed him for all those years. It gave him a fear of death. Once we realized what it was, we prayed it off, along with the fruit that came from it.

The next week, we were at Disneyland with the youth. Normally we didn't have to worry about Jason because he always stayed very close to us. We always knew right where he was. But that day, he wandered off and we didn't know where he had gone. He was totally set free of the fear in his life. Now we had to deal with fear, wondering where he was.

Of course, he was all right but we had to adjust to the change. To this day, he is fearless. But if we had not dealt with that fear when we did, he would still be living under it. He is now free.

There is no place in your life for discouragement or fear. They are things that will keep you from the confidence you need to boldly enter the promises that God has for you. That is why God commanded Joshua not to have either. They would have stopped him long before he took the entire land.

### Taking the Promised Land

We are going to talk more about how to get completely free of the curses that have prevented God's promises from flourishing in your life. But what we have covered so far is the foundation, the basic plan of action that you need to follow. These seven steps are what Joshua had to do and they are the same for us. They are an Old Testament picture of exactly what you must do to appropriate New Testament promises in your life. Let's review them before moving on.

**1. Die to the law and embrace grace.**

You cannot do it on your own merit. God wants you to live in the promises and the blessings, but it doesn't come because you deserve it or because you worked hard to get it. It comes because God, in His love for you, wants you to have it. It is available only through His grace by means of the blood of Jesus.

**2. Arise.**

You have to get your will involved. Just sitting there dreaming about the Promised Land won't get you where you need to go. You have to determine that you are going to take the promises. You're not going to be passive anymore. You're not going to blame others and you're not going to get mad at God. You are going to make a commitment and you're going to take what God has for you.

**3. Be strong and courageous.**

You can't be a wimp or a weakling or a victim. There are giants in the land who want to keep you from possessing it. But you can't be intimidated. You have to recognize that the devil is defeated and that you are going to push him off of what is your land.

**4. Know that God is with you.**

The Holy Spirit has partnered with you to stand against the enemy and take hold of the promises together with you. You are not alone. You have all the power of God to utilize in your battle. Learn to flow in the gifts of the Spirit. Make them a regular part of your life.

**5. Be obedient.**

Because so much depends on the Holy Spirit, decide to do things His way. Be quick to respond to His direction. He will tell you how to win and how to obtain the promise.

**6. Do not let the Word of God depart from your mouth, but meditate on it day and night.**

Talk God talk. Speak only what God says. Get the Word into your heart and your mind and your mouth. Learn it and constantly confess it and develop the thoughts of God.

**7. Do not be discouraged or fear.**

It is a command to put all discouragement and fear out of your life. It will rob you of energy and strength and it will cause you to take your foot off of the promises of God.

This was the foundation for victory that God laid out for Joshua to follow even before Israel ever crossed the Jordan River. It is the same plan that will work for you.

I know this because I have lived it. Tom and I started doing this in our thirties, over twenty-five years ago. Today we are prosperous, healthy and successful. Our marriage is strong. Our children are blessed and our ministry is effective around the world. But we had to get rid of some giants before we could experience that success.

We had to drive the giant of poverty out of our lives so that we could live in the wealth of the Kingdom today. And we didn't become wealthy through the ministry, either. God taught us how to invest and He blessed and directed all of our business dealings. But that couldn't happen until we drove out poverty.

There was divorce in both our families. If we hadn't driven out the divorce that was a part of our inheritance, we probably wouldn't be married today. We wouldn't be madly in love and best friends for over forty years.

We faced giants and we beat them. You can do the same. It's what God wants for you. He has given you freedom and prosperity and health and peace in the Promised Land. Now you need to take it.

# 5
## The Iniquities of Past Generations

I hope by now that you understand how important it is for you to stop sitting and doing nothing. The promises of God are there for you, but you have to possess them. You have to drive out the giants that are there and move into the Promised Land that God has for you. God provided life for Israel and set them free from the bondage of Egypt, but they still had to get up and leave. God provided the Promised Land, but they still had to cross the Jordan and move in. The same is true of you.

That doesn't mean that you won't face problems. Everyone does. We all have things that have held us back from the promises of God. We all have a past that we have to break free of in order to possess the land. No matter who you are, there are some giants in your Promised Land. We all came out of darkness and into the light of new life in Jesus.

But you had to come out of the darkness. You had to step into the light. There is a transition that has to take place. Paul wrote about it in Ephesians.

*And you He made alive, who were dead in*
*trespasses and sins, in which you once walked*

*according to the course of this world, accord-
ing to the prince of the power of the air, the
spirit who now works in the sons of disobedience.* (Ephesians 2:1-2)

The next verse makes it clear that all of us
had to be saved. We all lived in that former life.

*All of us also lived among them at one
time, gratifying the cravings of our sinful nature and following its desires and thoughts.*
(Ephesians 2:3 NIV)

No one can escape this. Before you became
born again, you were under the powers of darkness. We were all subject at one time to the kingdom of the enemy.

It is interesting that the kingdom of darkness
has a whole set of principles under which it operates.
And we were under those principles and obeyed
them. You have to understand that in the area of
your soul, in your personality, there were behaviors
that we all took on before we knew Jesus. You got
saved but you continued to operate in those personality behaviors. But God now wants you to be free.

The world system has given names to those
dysfunctional kinds of behavior. They are catego-
rized into the basic areas of victim, rescuer or enabler, and persecutor. They are not healthy. But

every one of us entered into one of those areas of behavior. You are not exempt.

You might have been a victim in life, which meant that you were always at the bottom. You always saw yourself as worthless. You always saw the glass half empty and everyone was always picking on you. If you were a victim, you wanted someone to take care of you and be responsible for you. You found your self-value in having someone else take on all of your responsibilities. As a result, you were totally consumed with yourself.

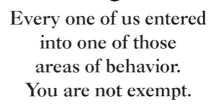

Every one of us entered into one of those areas of behavior. You are not exempt.

The enabler is often called codependent. He is a rescuer. He delights in taking on the responsibilities of the victim. He wants to be the hero, the savior. He finds his sense of self-value in helping others. The problem is that Jesus is the hero and He desires that the victim get better and learn to stand on his own in a healthy way. The enabler, on the other hand, can't bear to see the victim get better. If that happened, he would not be able to take care of him anymore, and then he would have nothing to make him feel valuable.

The persecutor represents the law. He passes judgment and then persecutes people, often through verbal or emotional attacks but frequently it turns into physical abuse. Persecutors are all black and white. They are hard and harsh and they hate victims. They are always finding fault with others and they condemn and try to make people worthless. They find their self-value by trying to show how inferior everyone else is to them.

As you grew up, you took on one of those types of wrong behavior. Most likely you had all three at one time or another, but there was probably one that dominated you most of the time. It became your identity. The problem is that as long as you identify with one of those dysfunctional behavior types, you will not experience all the blessings of the Promised Land. They are not healthy.

When we first started the church, we had someone in the congregation who worked in this area and he lovingly pointed out to Tom and me that we were enablers. We tried to take care of everybody. We had them lined up at the door of our house. They would come in and we would spend time praying with them, one after another after another.

There was a limit to how far the church could grow because we had all these victims and we only had time to take care of so many of them. It's good to help people but if they're not getting better and they have to keep coming back over and over with the same problems, then you're not really helping them. They don't want to get well.

They enjoy the attention they get when they are sick or oppressed and they want to use up all of your time.

I knew that in my family when I was growing up, I was the enabler. I was always trying to keep Daddy happy. He was a victim persecutor in our home. He was either physically abusing us or he was being the victim in life. Which meant that I was either the victim of the abuse or I was the rescuer trying to make him happy. Being a rescuer was something that went generations back for me. It was a generational curse. But I had to recognize that it was there and admit that it was a problem.

After our friend pointed it out to us, we said, "We don't want this in our lives." So we went on a four-day fast. We prayed together with a desire to get the dysfunction out of our lives.

And the Holy Spirit gave us an open vision. He showed us that the roles of victim, enabler and persecutor ran alongside the path of God. But they were not the path of God. They were the counterfeit. They are of this world and its system.

As you are walking through your Promised Land, you want to be sure that those things are not operating in your life. You don't want to live in denial. Stop saying, "I never did that," or "I never walked in that." We all have. We just read it in Ephesians 2:3. "All of us also lived among them at one time." Stop living in denial and get free of it.

If Tom and I had not taken the steps necessary to get free of that dysfunctional role of rescuer, the church would not be where it is today. Instead of 8,000 people, there would only be a few hundred because that is as many as we could have taken care of. We didn't realize at the time what the problem was, but as soon as it was pointed out to us, we dealt with it. And we don't have it in our lives anymore.

As a result, victims don't come to us. I used to be like a magnet for them. They knew that they would get all the attention they could want. But once I was free, they no longer felt compelled to connect to me. They either get free of being a victim or they go and look for someone who will take care of them and not expect them to change.

These counterfeits of the world system are addictive personality traits. They are things that are in the soul area, the personality area of your life. They will lock you into behavior patterns that will consistently prevent you from achieving your destiny. When Jesus gave you salvation, a significant part of that was setting your personality free so that you do not have to conform to those behaviors anymore. God wants you to be conformed to the image of Jesus, not the counterfeit of the world. You were made in His likeness and image. He wants you to be healthy in every part of your being, operating in the Kingdom of God. But as long as you hang onto that old baggage, you are not free to be what God called you to be.

**Generational Curses**

What causes us many of the problems that we face in getting free of wrong behaviors is that we don't recognize the real source from which they come. They often started long before you were even born. They are what we call generational curses.

A generational curse is in the soul or in the body. If there is an alcoholic father, then it tends to be passed down from generation to generation. When a person is violent, there is a greater likelihood that the children will be violent. My grandfather was very violent with my father. My father was then very violent in his family. When it came to my family, it was up to me to put that iniquity to a stop before it passed on to my children. I did that through fasting and prayer of repentance. Our family was set free. Now my children are not violent at all, but it had to be stopped before it got to them.

There are many things that we acknowledge are passed on in families. We are familiar with many generational traits. My father was married three times. In his second marriage, he had three children that I wasn't raised with even though I had spent a summer with them when they were young children. I was in my thirties before I ever really got acquainted with them. We went to stay with my father so we could get to know them.

It was interesting to see the generational traits in them. I could see myself in my sister, Diana. We

barely knew each other but she had similar personality traits. Some of her gestures were the same as
mine. We've all seen it and we always act surprised
when we see how much one of our children look or
act like their grandparents.

Various illnesses such as high blood pressure
or cancer can run in families. If you go to the doctor
with heart problems or mental illness or diabetes,
one of the first questions you will be asked is, "Does
this condition run in your family?" They can be and
are passed down from generation to generation.

The point is that these traits are not merely
genetic or learned behaviors. There is a spiritual
attachment that goes with sin and it can be passed
along from one generation to the next just as much
as how someone looks. These iniquities are generational curses.

When the Bible mentions iniquities, it is talking about generational curses that control the will.
They produce behavior that you don't know how
to get rid of. You don't want to do something but
you keep doing it anyway. It will continue to control you until you break that power by renouncing
it and putting the blood of Jesus over it. Only then
is the power broken and gone from your life. Only
then will you be able to prevent it from passing on
to your children.

We see this problem often in adoptions. The
behavioral problems that are sometimes seen in

adopted children are generational curses that come from the birth parents and which often baffle the adoptive parents. We had a man in the church some time ago who was adopted.

He came from a very re-sponsible family that was well-educated and free of any problems such as drug abuse. They did not want a child at the time, so they

—————❧—————
These traits are not merely genetic or learned behaviors. There is a spiritual attachment.

put him up for adoption. He grew up to be a very responsible and level-headed adult.

A couple of years after he was adopted, how-ever, his family adopted another boy. His new broth-er came from a very different background. It was a family that was very involved with drugs and alco-hol. They were homeless. They lived in the garbage and the addictions of the world. As soon as he was old enough, he started to get into trouble. He got onto drugs. He was always a victim in life and felt that life owed him something. He was always self-centered and grabbing, abusing the family and caus-ing much heartache. Today, he is in his forties and still having the same problems.

Both of these boys were adopted at a very young age and raised by the same parents. But they turned out very differently. The reason was the generational curses that were attached from birth. The new environment didn't get rid of the problems.

Only the blood of Jesus will set someone free from that kind of bondage.

If you have adopted children or are considering it, you should find out as much as you can about their background. If there are generational curses there, they will need to be broken or they will continue to affect that child's behavior for the rest of his life.

It is interesting that when Jesus dealt with people in bondage, he always looked to the parents. For example, it was Jairus who was asked to believe for the healing of his daughter, not the daughter (Mark 5:36). Remember the Syrophoenician woman who came to Jesus because her daughter was demon-possessed. It was not the daughter whose faith made the difference. It was the mother to whom Jesus said, "O woman, great is your faith! Let it be to you as you desire" (Matthew 15:28).

The point is that generational curses will create behavior in you that will control you until you break them. But they can be broken by the blood of Jesus and they need to be or they will pass on to your children. It is something that you cannot afford to ignore.

## 6
## Generational Sin Controls Our Will

Generational curses have the affect of violating your will. They cause you to do things that you don't want to do. I have seen it many times in ministry that people feel that they can't seem to control how they act and the problem is a generational curse.

I knew a girl who couldn't stand to be around anything that had a sexual connotation to it. Even seeing other people kissing would trigger something in her. It was as though a force came over her and she wanted to abandon her family, her children, even her faith. She felt compelled to run after sexual perversion and prostitution. It wasn't what she wanted but it controlled her.

As she began to share this with me, we realized that it was a generational curse, an iniquity of the forefathers. Her forefathers had been involved in sexual perversions, including rape, and that curse had attached itself to later generations, including her. It was violating her will.

We prayed and asked God to forgive her forefathers and her. We put the blood of Jesus over the situation. We saw the curse nailed to the cross. And the power of that curse was completely broken. She was delivered of it and never experienced that violation of her will again.

### What I Want To Do, I Do Not Do

The apostle Paul understood the effects of past iniquities. He experienced the same inability to overcome them that we all have felt. He wanted to do one thing but ended up doing something else.

> *I do not understand what I do. For what I want to do I do not do, but what I hate I do.* (Romans 7:15 NIV)

When you are in the grip of an iniquity, a generational curse, you don't understand what you are doing. You don't know why you are doing it and, when you are born again and Spirit-filled, you hate it. You feel like you have no control over it.

Before I got married I never dreamed I had a problem with anger. I was easy-going and well-respected. I was a cheerleader in high school, on student council, always on the honor role, teacher's pet—everything that would indicate that I was level-headed and self-controlled.

Then I got married. We started to establish our home life, but I had all that baggage from my childhood. The anger that had been there in my father and my grandfather somehow found its way into my home. Two weeks into the marriage I was throwing ice cream at Tom.

I couldn't believe I did that. It wasn't long, though, before it became obvious that something was there that I couldn't control. It was horrible. I did everything I knew to be spiritual. I spent all day with God and the moment Tom walked in the house, this anger would come over me.

Like Paul, I couldn't understand the things I did. Then I would consider that I was born again, Spirit-filled and I loved God. I spent all day with Him, praying and studying. And it seemed that even God couldn't help me. I didn't know what to do.

> I had never been angry before. So I went into denial and claimed it wasn't my fault.

I didn't realize that I was dealing with a generational curse, an iniquity. I had never even heard of that. I thought it must be all Tom's fault. I had never been angry before. So I went into denial and claimed it wasn't my fault.

In a sense, I was right. I really didn't have any control over it. Of course, I was still responsible. But I was also helpless—again, just like Paul. It was violating my will.

> *And if I do what I do not want to do, I agree that the law is good. As it is, it is no longer I myself who do it, but it is sin living*

*in me. I know that nothing good lives in me, that is, in my sinful nature. For I have the desire to do what is good, but I cannot carry it out. For what I do is not the good I want to do; no, the evil I do not want to do—this I keep on doing. Now if I do what I do not want to do, it is no longer I who do it, but it is sin living in me that does it.* (Romans 7:16-20 NIV)

Anyone who has tried in their own strength to get free of a generational curse can understand the cry of Paul just a couple of verses later.

*What a wretched man I am! Who will rescue me from this body of death?* (Romans 7:24 NIV)

In the next verse, Paul answers his own question. The answer, of course, is Jesus.

*Thanks be to God—through Jesus Christ our Lord!* (Romans 7:25 NIV)

That was the answer in Paul's life and it was the answer in my life. First I had to admit that there was a problem. Finally one day, Tom came home and I said, "I think I have an anger problem."

He agreed with me, which was not surprising at that point. But he said the one thing that we needed to do. "We're going to go on a three-day fast."

As we saw earlier, the Holy Spirit partners with us to help us in our weakness. The gifts of the Spirit are in us. The Spirit is ready to show us how to fight the battle and win. And that is exactly what happened to me. We recognized the iniquity, saw it nailed to the cross, and the blood of Jesus completely broke that generational curse. It has not been a part of my life now for over thirty years.

In Christ, we are a new creation. We do not identify any longer with the curse of the past. It is important that you develop this self-awareness. You are born again. You are in the family of God. You are no longer defined by the sin that lives in you. You are now identified by the Spirit of God who dwells in you.

For Tom, the generational curse was poverty. I mentioned earlier that he grew up in extreme poverty. He lived in fear of poverty. Five years after we got saved, we were so poor that we didn't even own a car. That generational curse would not let us prosper.

But once he realized that God said he was to be prosperous, we looked up all the Scriptures that pertained to prosperity and began to quote them several times a day. We made a tape of them and played it all day. Tom had to stop identifying with the poverty and step out of it. Tom had to recognize that it was a generational curse.

I had an anger problem that came from my father and his father, but I never struggled with poverty. It was not part of the iniquity of my ancestors. That part was easy for me. My inheritance was wealth. My grandfather on my mother's side was an interior decorator and he was wealthy. My grandfather on my father's side was so wealthy that my father was raised with maids and butlers. It was easy for me to believe for prosperity, even though I wasn't raised with prosperity.

But Tom's heritage had been poverty. He had to learn to think differently so that he didn't identify with it anymore. That's where God's promises came in. For the first several months, it seemed like he was dealing with it every five minutes. The thoughts of poverty would flood over him, and he would call it sin and repent. He recognized it as sin that lived in him and he kept at it until the curse was broken. Now he can say that poverty has not been a part of his life for over thirty years.

But the first thing that Tom had to do was recognize where that curse came from. As we began praying about it, the Holy Spirit showed Tom that it went back to his ancestors. It was sin dwelling in him—sin that came from his father and his father's father. It was a generational curse. It had nothing to

do with how hard he worked. Tom worked very hard. His father worked hard. His grandfather worked hard. But they were still poor. It had nothing to do with how smart they were.
Tom's father was a bril-
liant man. Tom is a brilliant
man. But the poverty was
still there until Tom recognized it for what it was and
claimed the power of the

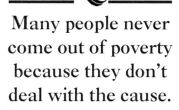

Many people never come out of poverty because they don't deal with the cause.

blood of Jesus to break it. Now Tom is called to mentor the body of Christ to step into great wealth.

Many people never come out of poverty because they don't deal with the cause. They don't understand that it comes from a generational curse. You need the Holy Spirit to partner with you to break it. Living with the curse is not God's way. When God gives you the promise and you bind yourself to it, you confess everything that argrees with it as the truth and you confess anything that disagrees with it as sin. You put your foot on the promise and the Holy Spirit will show you the right way to go. He will reveal to you the source of the curse in your life, and He will direct you so that you can be rid of it forever. Let the gifts of the Spirit flow freely, and you'll hear a voice telling you, "No, this is not the way. Walk here instead."

It is very important that you embrace the Holy Spirit with God's Word and let Him lead you. He is ready to give you a word of knowledge, a word of wisdom or a dream. He'll give you a vision, healing, a miracle—whatever you need to break the curse in your life. Remember that you don't need to go looking for sin. You do need to desire the Holy Spirit. If there is sin that you need to worry about, He will show you.

Iniquities must be dealt with. You cannot afford to ignore them and let them hang around.

> *And those of you who are left shall waste away*
> *in their iniquity in your enemies' lands;*
> *also in their fathers' iniquities, which are*
> *with them, they shall waste away.*
> *But if they confess their iniquity and the iniquity*
> *of their fathers, with their unfaithfulness in*
> *which they were unfaithful to Me, and that*
> *they also have walked contrary to Me,*
> *and that I also have walked contrary to them*
> *and have brought them into the land of*
> *their enemies;*
> *if their uncircumcised hearts are humbled,*
> *and they accept their guilt—*
> *then I will remember My covenant with Ja-*
> *cob, and My covenant with Isaac and My*
> *covenant with Abraham I will remember;*
> *I will remember the land.*
>                                     (Leviticus 26:39-42)

This says clearly that they would waste away because of the iniquities of their fathers. To waste away means to dwindle, to rot, to decay in the land of the enemy. When you are under a curse, it just keeps coming. A family that is under a curse will keep experiencing disaster after disaster until they deal with the source of the problem. It has dominion over their lives.

But Leviticus gives the solution. It says to "confess their iniquity and the iniquity of their fathers, with their unfaithfulness in which they were unfaithful to Me." Confession is absolutely essential. You have to get to the point where you say, "I will not make any more excuses. I will not live in denial anymore. I'll recognize that this area of my life is not blessed, and I will humble myself and accept the guilt and repent."

God declares that when you do that, He will remember His covenant with you and He will bring you into the Land of Promise. He will deliver you from the curse and give you complete victory so that it never bothers you again.

1 Samuel describes a generational curse as something that lasts forever. This verse is a prophecy against the house of Eli.

*Behold, the days are coming that I will cut off your arm and the arm of your father's house, so that there will not be an*

*old man in your house. And you will see
an enemy in My dwelling place, despite all
the good which God does for Israel. And
there shall not be an old man in your house
forever.* (1 Samuel 2:31-32)

In Deuteronomy, it talks about a generational curse that lasts for ten generations.

*One of illegitimate birth shall not enter
the assembly of the LORD; even to the tenth
generation none of his descendants shall enter the assembly of the LORD. An Ammonite
or Moabite shall not enter the assembly of the
LORD; even to the tenth generation none of his
descendants shall enter the assembly of the
LORD forever.* (Deuteronomy 23:2-3)

Exodus 34:7 speaks of generational curses, though it is usually not quoted in that con-
text. It says that the iniquities of the fathers are
visited on the children to the third and fourth
generation.

*The LORD, the LORD God, merciful and gra-
cious, longsuffering, and abounding in good-
ness and truth, keeping mercy for thousands,
forgiving iniquity and transgression and sin,
by no means clearing the guilty, visiting the*

*iniquity of the fathers upon the children and the children's children to the third and fourth generation.* (Exodus 34:6-7)

Exodus 20:5 says the same thing, but adds a statement that God would much rather give generational blessings than allow the curse to continue.

*For I, the LORD your God, am a jealous God, visiting the iniquity of the fathers upon the children to the third and fourth generations of those who hate Me, but showing mercy to thousands, to those who love Me and keep My commandments.* (Exodus 20:5-6)

Once we got free of poverty in our lives, the curse stopped. It no longer had any hold on our children. Instead, we passed the blessing on to them. Our children are naturally blessed. Prosperity just comes their way. Whatever their hands touch prospers. They buy stock and it goes up. We broke the curse in our lives and our children received the blessings.

We are first-generation Christians so there was a lot that we needed to get rid of in our lives. But as the Holy Spirit revealed those things to us, we confessed them as sin and got rid of them. Our lives today are nothing like thirty years ago. We are blessed in every area. The curse is broken.

Iniquities are passed down from generation to generation until the curse is broken. In Romans, Paul said that sin came into the world through one man (Romans 5:12) and death came through sin. The curse got passed from one generation to the next all the way down to where we live. All mankind suffered because of Adam's sin. But then Jesus stepped into the picture and the curse of death was broken. In Christ, we now pass the blessing from generation to generation. Jesus paid the penalty of our iniquities in full and we have been set free. Now it's up to us to take what Jesus has done and get it working in our lives.

# 7

# The Cross in the Old Testament

The cross of Jesus and His death and resurrection were foreshadowed throughout the Old Testament. A graphic example is in the story of Joshua. We have already seen that God gave Joshua specific instructions for conquering the Promised Land. God gave it to him, but he still had to drive out the giants who lived there. We saw that this was a picture of the promises God has for us and that we have to take possession of those promises by driving out the generational curses that block our blessings.

As Joshua gained victory over those enemies, we see a picture of our victory through the cross. Joshua 10 describes one of the climactic battles of the campaign to take the Promised Land. Joshua faced five Amorite kings and God gave him complete victory over them. The kings fled and tried to hide in a cave, but the Israelites found them and trapped them there until Joshua arrived. We can see from this incident just how Joshua treated the enemies who tried to keep him from the Promises of God.

*So it was, when they brought out those kings to Joshua, that Joshua called for all the men*

*of Israel, and said to the captains of the men
of war who went with him, "Come near, put
your feet on the necks of these kings." And they
drew near and put their feet on their necks.
Then Joshua said to them, "Do not be afraid,
nor be dismayed; be strong and of good courage,
for thus the LORD will do to all your enemies
against whom you fight." (Joshua 10:24-25)*

Putting their feet on the necks of their enemies represented breaking the power, the authority of the generational curses that lived in the land. Once the victory was displayed, Joshua completely eliminated them. It was a picture of Jesus defeating Satan and taking his power of attorney away from him. It was a fulfillment of the picture in Genesis 3:15 where Jesus would crush the head of the serpent.

*And afterward Joshua struck them and
killed them, and hanged them on five trees,
and they were hanging on the trees until evening. (Joshua 10:26)*

Joshua identified the five kings as curses when he hung them on trees. He foreshadowed Jesus becoming a curse for us by hanging on the cross for us and defeating generational curses in our lives. Five is the number that symbolically represents grace. In dealing with the five enemies, we see the grace of

God at work in the life of Israel. Joshua crucified the generational curses that blocked the blessings. Then he buried them in the cave.

> *So it was at the time of the going down of the sun that Joshua commanded, and they took them down from the trees, cast them into the cave where they had been hidden, and laid large stones against the cave's mouth, which remain until this very day.* (Joshua 10:27)

Remember that Deuteronomy said the bodies were not to be left on the tree after dark or the land would be defiled. That is why Joshua took them down at sunset. That was the same reason Jesus had to be buried before nightfall. The kings were buried in a cave and large stones rolled over the mouth. This foreshadowed the day when Jesus would be buried in a cave and a large stone rolled over the entrance. The execution of the five Amorite kings was

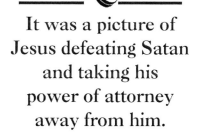

It was a picture of Jesus defeating Satan and taking his power of attorney away from him.

a picture of the importance that the cross of Calvary would play in getting rid of the generational curses that block us from the Promises of God.

It is amazing how often the picture of the cross occurs in the Old Testament. Joshua began

the practice of hanging his enemies on a tree from
the very beginning of the conquest of the Promised
Land. That is what he did with the first king that
he captured.

> *And the king of Ai he hanged on a tree un-*
> *til evening. And as soon as the sun was down,*
> *Joshua commanded that they should take his*
> *corpse down from the tree, cast it at the en-*
> *trance of the gate of the city, and raise over it*
> *a great heap of stones that remains to this day.*
> (Joshua 8:29)

When Joshua looked at his enemies, he saw
them as curses and he treated them accordingly. He
hung them on a tree and made sure that all of Israel saw them as defeated and gone. Then he buried them. That is the same way that we have to
deal with the generational curses that block our entrance to the blessings of God. We have to see them
as nailed to the cross, dead and gone.

> *And you, being dead in your trespasses and*
> *the uncircumcision of your flesh, He has made*
> *alive together with Him, having forgiven you*
> *all trespasses, having wiped out the handwrit-*
> *ing of requirements that was against us, which*
> *was contrary to us. And He has taken it out of*
> *the way, having nailed it to the cross, having*

*disarmed the principalities and powers, He made a public spectacle of them, triumphing over them in it.* (Colossians 2:13-15)

### The Bronze Serpent

The cross was foreshadowed in other ways also. In fact, everything God did in the Old Testament pointed toward the cross. We shouldn't be surprised since it is the focal point of redemption. All of history centered on that moment when Jesus was crucified.

> Everything God did in the Old Testament pointed toward the cross.

In Numbers 21, the Israelites were afflicted by fiery serpents. Many died from the poisonous bites. They cried out to God for deliverance from that curse. So God instructed Moses to make a serpent out of bronze.

> *Then the LORD said to Moses, "Make a fiery serpent, and set it on a pole; and it shall be that everyone who is bitten, when he looks at it, shall live." So Moses made a bronze serpent, and put it on a pole; and so it was, if a serpent had bitten anyone, when he looked at the bronze serpent, he lived.* (Numbers 21:8-9)

Some translators say, "he shall be healed." The pole was a picture of the cross. The serpent represented the curse. For Israel, the curse was the bite of poisonous snakes. For you, it might be that you've been bitten by cancer or some sickness or some other curse operating in your life.

All of the Israelites were children of God. But those who refused to look at the cross when they were bitten with the curse still died from it. Those who saw the curse hanging on the cross were healed and lived. The power of the curse was broken.

Jesus referred to this picture of the cross and related it to His own death.

> *And as Moses lifted up the serpent in the wilderness, even so must the Son of Man be lifted up.* (John 3:14)

Jesus had to become the curse for us by hanging on the cross. He returned to the same image again a few chapters later.

> *Then Jesus said to them, "When you lift up the Son of Man, then you will know that I am He."* (John 8:28)

And again in chapter 12.

*And I, if I am lifted up from the earth, will draw all peoples to Myself.* (John 12:32)

It is the cross that sets us free from generational curses.  As we see the curse nailed there, the power that it had over us is completely broken.

### Getting Rid of Iniquities

In the Old Testament, generational curses are referred to as iniquities.  Iniquities are passed down from generation to generation.  That is why we call them generational curses.  They keep us from experiencing the blessings of the Promised Land that God intends for us.  Iniquities are blessings blockers.

There is only one way to get rid of iniquities.  You have to nail them to the cross.  Nothing else will break a curse in your life.  It was in the suffering and death of Jesus that your iniquities were broken from your life.  The stories of Joshua and Moses picture the cross, but Isaiah directly prophesied about it.

*But He was wounded for our transgressions,*
*He was bruised for our iniquities;*
*The chastisement for our peace was upon*
   *Him,*
*And by His stripes we are healed.*
                        (Isaiah 53:5)

"Transgression" mean rebellion to God's authority, a rejection of God's will in your life. Iniquities are generational curses. The next few verses describe the suffering that Jesus would endure for our deliverance. Verse 11 again states that He will bear our iniquities.

> *He shall see the labor of His soul and be satisfied.*
> *By His knowledge My righteous Servant shall justify many,*
> *For He shall bear their iniquities.*
> (Isaiah 53:11)

Jesus justified many by hanging on the cross. This was the labor of His soul. It is by the cross that we have been set free of generational curses. Jesus dealt with the penalty of all sins and all iniquities. He was beaten and nailed to the cross. He went to hell for us and was resurrected. The penalty was paid in full. The New Testament tells us that Jesus actually became a curse for us.

> *Christ has redeemed us from the curse of the law, having become a curse for us (for it is written, "Cursed is everyone who hangs on a tree")* (Galatians 3:13)

In this verse, the apostle Paul quotes from the Old Testament law.

> *If a man has committed a sin deserving of death, and you hang him on a tree, his body shall not remain overnight on the tree, but you shall surely bury him that day, so that you do not defile the land which the* LORD *your God is giving you as an inheritance, for he who is hanged is accursed of God.* (Deuteronomy 21:22-23)

We need to understand the significance of the cross. When Jesus was hung on the cross, He became a curse to God. That was why He had to hang on the cross. He took on the curse.

Next, understand that when God sees the crucifixion, He sees us as crucified with Jesus.

> *For if we have been united together in the likeness of His death, certainly we also shall be in the likeness of His resurrection, knowing this, that our old man was crucified with Him, that the body of sin might be done away with, that we should no longer be slaves of sin.* (Romans 6:5-6)

When God looks at the cross, He sees Jesus the head and us, mankind, the body, united in death.

But He also then sees us alive with Jesus in resurrection. God sees generational curses as nailed to the cross and done away with.

Now it is up to us to receive that into our lives. We have to see generational curses the same way God does—nailed to the cross of Calvary.

When the enemy inflicted rheumatoid arthritis on my body, this was how I had to deal with it. I had the severe crippling kind. There is no cure for it and it was working fast. I could barely walk. The doctor said I'd be in a wheelchair in two weeks.

But I understood breaking generational curses. I knew about the cross. I got up early in the morning and began to quote the Word. I saw myself doing all the things that I couldn't do—running, jumping, skiing, riding a bike. Then I pictured the word "rheumatoid arthritis" and I saw it nailed to the cross. I saw it as something that Jesus dealt with just as Paul said it. I saw myself alive and free in Christ.

> *And you, being dead in your trespasses and the uncircumcision of your flesh, He has made alive together with Him, having forgiven you all trespasses, having wiped out the handwriting of requirements that was against us, which was contrary to us. And He has taken it out of the way, having nailed it to the cross.*

*Having disarmed principalities and powers,*
*He made a public spectacle of them, triumph-*
*ing over them in it.* (Colossians 2:13-15)

Within two months I was totally healed. The
doctors couldn't believe it. They had run all kinds of
tests and had me going to a specialist and then sud-
denly it was gone. More than a dozen years later, it's
still gone. The power of that curse was completely
broken in my life. It was nailed to the cross.

## 8
## The Power of the Cross

I recall a situation in which a woman began to experience a problem in her thirties. It was as though a force came over her and put her into a deep, deep depression, even though she knew Jesus. When it happened, she just couldn't seem to get herself out of it. It was like she fell into a big black hole and she felt as though she was drowning.

As we talked, I asked her if there was any history of depression in her parents. She told me that her father had suffered from mental illness. He was diagnosed with manic depression and he was bipolar. He had gotten a medical discharge from the service because of it. The depression that she suffered from was an attempt of the enemy to put that same curse on her so that it would continue to be there in the next generation.

We began to pray. We asked God to forgive the forefathers and to forgive her. We saw the curse nailed to the cross and the power of depression completely broken. We saw the blood of Jesus over her. The power of the cross and the blood of Jesus completely set her free from that curse. It went away and it never came back. There is no more mental illness in her family.

The image of the cross appears throughout the Old Testament because it is the single most important part of redemption. Everything in the Old Testament looked forward to the death and resurrection of Jesus. Without the cross, we cannot get free of the generational curses in our lives. That is where we have to start.

Once you understand that, you are ready to move into the Promises of God and overcome and destroy the obstacles to your blessing. Over the next few chapters, we will look at five steps that you need to take to fully experience the power of the cross in your life.

**Fellowship at the Cross**

It is important to recognize how powerful the cross is, but then you need to tap into that power. Paul called it fellowshipping with Christ's suffering. That means that he identified with Jesus' death and with what Jesus accomplished on the cross.

> *... that I may know Him and the power of His resurrection, and the fellowship of His sufferings.* (Philippians 3:10)

What does it mean to suffer with Him? It means to identify with His suffering. It doesn't mean that you now have to suffer. Jesus already did that so that you don't have to. Suffering with

Him means spending time fellowshipping with Him at the cross and seeing the curse nailed there.

I am living proof that this works. I saw rheumatoid arthritis nailed to the cross, and its power over me was broken. My husband, Tom, had throat cancer. We saw it nailed to the cross and its power over him was broken.

So often we don't see miracles and healing in our lives. We don't see the blessings that God has for us. It is because we fail to take on what Jesus did for us on the cross and the blessing blockers stay where they keep us from God's best. We don't deal with generational curses,

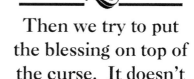

Then we try to put the blessing on top of the curse. It doesn't work that way.

and then we try to put the blessing on top of the curse. It doesn't work that way. We have to see the power of the cross and receive it into our lives. Then the blessing can flow freely to us.

In the Gospels, we see the cross from the perspective of mankind. When we look at the cross, we see Jesus and His suffering for us.

In the epistles, however, we see the cross from God's perspective. When He looks at the cross, He sees Maureen Anderson crucified. He sees you crucified. When Jesus was crucified, I was crucified with Him. I hung on the cross with Him. When God looks at the cross, He sees us crucified with Jesus.

Our old nature, all the sins, the transgressions and the iniquities were hung on the cross with Christ. The price for those iniquities was paid in full. The old man is dead. This is how God sees the cross.

*Knowing this, that our old man was cruci-fied with Him, that the body of sin might be done away with, that we should no longer be slaves of sin.* (Romans 6:6)

We know this by fellowshipping at the cross. The reason it is so important to know this and to see it is because that is how generational curses are broken. They are put to death. They have been crucified so that we can be free of them.

*For he who has died has been freed from sin. Now if we died with Christ, we believe that we shall also live with Him, knowing that Christ, having been raised from the dead, dies no more. Death no longer has dominion over Him.* (Romans 6:7-8)

I now live in a resurrected life. Not only did I hang on the cross with Jesus, not only were my iniquities paid in full, but I died with Him. I was buried in that tomb with Him. I went to hell with Him. And I was resurrected with Him. When Jesus was resurrected, you were resurrected, too.

Jesus did His part. He died and was resurrected. Now you have to do your part. Remember how God gave Israel the Promised Land but they still had to possess it? They still had to drive out the giants. You have life and freedom through the power of the cross, but you still have to come into agreement with what Jesus did. God sees every one of us set free, but we have to do our part. We have to see those things nailed to the cross.

> *And you, being dead in your trespasses and the uncircumcision of your flesh, He has made alive together with Him, having forgiven you all trespasses, having wiped out the handwriting of requirements that was against us, which was contrary to us. And He has taken it out of the way, having nailed it to the cross. Having disarmed principalities and powers, He made a public spectacle of them, triumphing over them in it.* (Colossians 2:13-15)

Through the cross, those giants who opposed you were made powerless. They have no more power in your life. The were disarmed. They no longer have any weapons that will work against you.

Those giants who have blocked your blessings have been made into a public spectacle. At the cross, you have triumphed over them. The victory is at the cross.

Every time I have had to deal with something that had power in my life, something that was impossible in the natural, I have seen it nailed to the cross. When I see it nailed to the cross, it becomes powerless.

If you have been united in His death, then you are united in His resurrection. If you see yourself crucified with Him, you can see yourself resurrected with Him.

Too often we want to forget about the cross. We just want the blessings. But if we don't recognize what happened at the cross, we can't live in the blessing. We have to fellowship at the cross with His suffering and what He did. We have to acknowledge it and appreciate it.

In Romans, Paul calls us joint heirs with Christ. He is the anointed one and we are partners with Him.

> *The Spirit Himself bears witness with our spirit that we are children of God, and if children, then heirs—heirs of God and joint heirs with Christ, if indeed we suffer with Him, that we may also be glorified together.* (Romans 8:17)

What does it mean to be an heir? Everything that is God's is now yours. And He owns everything. He gave everything to His son, Jesus, and you are a joint heir with Him. You are a partner. When He suffered, you died with Him and now you share in the glory of resurrection as well.

When it says, "if we indeed suffer with Him," it does not mean that we now have to go through some kind of suffering. Fellowship with His suffering means that you acknowledge His suffering at the cross and you see that Jesus paid it all for you. If you come into agreement with that, then you will be glorified with Him.

# 9

# The Holy Spirit's Battle Plan

As Israel came out of Egypt, they were not pre-pared to move right into the Promised Land. They still argued with God and they kept looking back at how life had been in Egypt, remembering the good and completely forgetting about how hard their lives had been as slaves.

The trip from Egypt to the Promised Land was not a very long distance. To walk straight through, it only required a couple of weeks. Yet Israel took forty years to cover that short distance. There was a lot of baggage in their thinking that had to be dealt with. They had to learn to trust God and let the Holy Spirit direct them.

We all have plenty of baggage when we are born again. You brought in baggage from your forefathers, from your family, things you believed that were not in line with God's Word, attitudes that you collected. Now you want to enter the Land of Promise and you have all these things that stand in your way and cause you problems. And as a result, it takes you far longer to experience the blessings than it needs to.

The problem is that we usually have so much baggage that we don't know where to start. If we had to do it all at once, it would overwhelm us. So God deals with it one part at a time.

This was what He told Moses. He would not give Israel the entire Promised Land all at once.

> *I will not drive them out from before you in one year, lest the land become desolate and the beasts of the field become too numerous for you. Little by little I will drive them out from before you, until you have increased, and you inherit the land.* (Exodus 23:29-30)

And that is what happened. Joshua conquered the land in a very orderly way. If you draw his progress on a map, you can see that it was not a haphazard, unplanned advance into the Promised Land. Each step made sense. There was a plan to it.

First Israel had to secure a crossing place along the Jordan. Since the nations living there wouldn't allow them to pass, they began by defeating the two Amorite kings, Sihon and Og. That gave them safe territory on the east side of the Jordan River. In fact, two and a half of the tribes decided to settle there.

Next they crossed the Jordan and set up a base at Gilgal and conducted the rest of the campaign from there. That was necessary so that they didn't have to take all of their possessions with them into battle.

The first city they took, Jericho, was located at a place that blocked access to the rest of the southern part of the land. It wasn't by accident that God directed Joshua there. Jericho had to be conquered first.

After Jericho, Joshua dealt with the other kings in the southern part of the Promised Land that were the greatest threat. Then, when that area was secure, he turned to the north and conquered the most important areas there. Only when all of the major threats had been eliminated did Joshua divide the land up between the tribes and send them out to take care of the remaining pockets of resistance.

> Joshua conquered the land in a very orderly way.

It was not just a matter of attacking wherever they felt like. Joshua moved according to a plan and he took the land a little at a time. What is most important is the fact that the plan came from the Holy Spirit. Every step of the way, Joshua looked to God to show him what to attack next.

There were only two times that he did not ask God first and both times he got into trouble. The first was when he sent men to attack Ai. Because of the sin of Achan at Jericho, the attack was defeated. After they sought God's direction, they had victory. The second time was the treaty with the Gibeonites. They didn't ask God first and the result was a bad treaty that they had to live with.

In every case where Joshua got the battle plan from the Holy Spirit, he was victorious. The second step, then, in experiencing the power of the cross is to let the Holy Spirit show you the battle plan. Let Him reveal problems to you one at a time. Then, as He shows you, deal with them.

When the Holy Spirit shows me what I need to fight, I start addressing that situation. He shows me a generational iniquity that has power in my life and then I start to deal with it. Little by little, He'll take off one layer at a time. God develops in me what I need to correct that situation and then He'll take another layer. Sometimes it takes a year from the beginning of a battle until it is totally ended and I'm in complete possession of the land. But then I'm able to walk in what I've conquered in my life.

Don't become sin conscious in this process. Keep your eyes on Jesus, who is the Word of God. Meditate on what God says. Quote the Word of God. Keep the Word in your mouth. Stay focused on the blessings and the promises. The Holy Spirit is faithful to bring up those things in your life that disagree with the Word and when He does, see them nailed to the cross. Renounce them and the Holy Spirit will give you something to fill in that area that will make you more Christ-like.

The Holy Spirit will bring you into the blessings of God one step at a time as you keep your eyes on God's Word. Often, when we see a situation in our lives, it is like a frightening monster that is too big to handle so we become afraid or discouraged. But any problem can be overcome. You do it the same way that you eat an elephant—one bite at a time.

Just remember that the Holy Spirit has the plan already figured out. Don't be discouraged. Don't get dismayed. Don't be full of fear. Keep listening to the Holy Spirit and don't quit, and one day, you'll find that you've taken over the Promised Land and the blessings are yours.

*Damaged DNA*

# 10
## Embrace Change

The flesh hates change. We like our baggage even though we hate it. We like to keep going around the same mountain for years at a time because we know the path so well. We stay in the desert because we know right where every rock and thorn bush is. There's nothing growing there but at least we know our way around. We don't want to change, even though we hate where we are. It's too familiar.

But change brings maturity. The third step in experiencing the power of the cross is to be willing to change.

The first thing most people do when confronted with the need to change is to go into denial. "Oh, I don't have that problem. It's not my situation." It's as though your house is burning down and nothing inside you says that there is an emergency. Denial paralyzes you and says everything is fine when it isn't. Denial is a thief to dreams and to blessings.

I know a person who lived in denial. One morning her husband left for a breakfast appointment but never arrived at the destination. When he didn't show up, his appointment called but, though she didn't know where he was, she still didn't respond. Instead, she went about her day as if everything was fine.

The man's assistant tried to find him. She called the hospital and discovered that he was in the emergency room with a kidney stone. Once they found that information, his office called her and let her know where he was. She still acted like everything was normal. It was a friend from work who went to the hospital and sat with him all through that evening and then brought him home from the hospital.

After that incident, she realized that she had a real denial problem. Nothing inside of her said "emergency." It wasn't that there was a problem with their marriage. She loved him very much, but she was in denial about the situation. When her husband got home that night he said, "I'm afraid that if I die, you won't show up for the funeral." It was only then that she decided to deal with the problem.

I've seen denial happen frequently with sickness. The doctor said the disease is there. The tests show it as being there. But they still say, "I don't have it." They think they are exercising faith by refusing to acknowledge that they are sick.

But denial is not faith. It is just denial. Faith faces the issue head on. People in denial try to run from the problem, hoping it will go away if they pretend it doesn't exist. They make themselves very, very busy so that they never have to think about the problem. They don't want to make any changes. This is what many people that I have known over the years have done. But their denial means that the disease is raging inside of them and nothing is fighting it. It progresses completely unchecked.

> Denial is not faith. It is just denial. Faith faces the issue head on.

Denial actually stops your dreams. Every one of us faces challenges along the path to the Promised Land that have to be overcome if we are to get there. If you ignore those obstacles, you won't get around them. The giants in the land are real. You can't defeat them by ignoring them. You have to meet them head on with the power of the Word, the Holy Spirit and the blood of Jesus. If you don't, you will not reach your dreams.

For the same reason, denial stops the victory. Too often, people think that the way to breaking free of any bondage is to pretend that it doesn't exist. As a result, they struggle with it for their whole lives. Denial keeps them from dealing directly with the problem. It keeps us in bondage.

There is a battle to be won. To win it, you will have to make some changes. If you don't change, then neither will the situation. Faith is not ignoring the problem. Faith confronts it and wins.

What is faith, then? Faith is seeing something already done. You admit the situation is there, but you see it nailed to the cross. You begin to speak the Word. You pray the Word. You confess it. You walk in it. You see yourself doing the things that they said you couldn't do. With faith, you change the situation, but you don't deny it. Faith requires that you change.

Change begins when you can admit that you have a problem. You ask the Holy Spirit to show you the battle plan. If five different people tell you that you have a problem, then you probably do. Admit it.

Denial will always keep you in darkness. It causes you to withdraw, to get busy and to ignore it. You will never change in denial.

God intends for us to be free of the problems that come from the curse.

> *For the law of the Spirit of life in Christ Jesus has made me free from the law of sin and death.* (Romans 8:2)

So we are free from the law of sin, the penalty of sin that brings death. Life comes by the Spirit.

*For if you live according to the flesh you will die; but if by the Spirit you put to death the deeds of the body, you will live.* (Romans 8:13)

If you live in denial and you resist change and you resist dealing with your situation, you'll die. Change is vital. Look at the same verse in the Amplified Bible.

*For if you live according to [the dictates of] the flesh, you will surely die. But if through the power of the [Holy] Spirit you are [habitually] putting to death (making extinct, deadening) the [evil] deeds prompted by the body, you shall [really and genuinely] live forever.* (Romans 8:13 AMP)

I know I'm born again of the Spirit of God when I receive Christ Jesus, but now it's up to me to acknowledge when the Holy Spirit is showing me something that needs to be put to death. How we listen to the Holy Spirit will determine how effectively we move into the blessings that God has for us. Paul told Timothy that there are two kinds of people. He likened them to vessels.

*But in a great house there are not only vessels of gold and silver, but also of wood and clay, some for honor and some for dishonor. Therefore if anyone cleanses himself from the latter, he will be a vessel for honor, sanctified and useful for the master, prepared for every good work.* (2 Timothy 2:20-21)

To be a vessel for honor, you must cleanse the dishonor, the garbage, from your life. That means that when the Holy Spirit shows you something that needs to be cleansed, you can't go into denial and resist it. You have to let the Holy Spirit show it to you so that you can take it to the cross. You have to be ready to say, "Holy Spirit, show me the battle plan. I'm going to cleanse my house of this. I'm going to be a vessel of honor fit for the master's use. I will keep maturing and growing in God. I will change."

Allow the Holy Spirit to show you those things that are blocking your blessing, those things that are hindering you. Get rid of them.

*Therefore we also, since we are surrounded by so great a cloud of witnesses, let us lay aside every weight, and the sin which so easily ensnares us, and let us run with endurance the race that is set before us.* (Hebrews 12:1)

All kinds of things can hinder us from the life God plans for us. But the power of the cross will overcome every obstacle. Jesus has already done it.

Every victory in your life is already won. You just have to claim it and receive it and then partner with the Holy Spirit as you walk it through.

Twenty years ago, my husband, Tom, went skiing with our boys. He fell and broke some ribs but he still kept skiing the rest of the day. Over the next few weeks, he kept complaining about how tired and weak he felt. He knew something wasn't right.

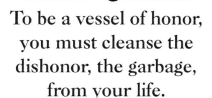

To be a vessel of honor, you must cleanse the dishonor, the garbage, from your life.

Finally he went to the doctor. They ran tests and discovered that the strain of skiing with his injury had brought on a mild heart attack.

That was something that could have been a great hindrance to us if we had allowed it to. But that same night, when we got home, we put on some Gloria Copeland healing tapes and listened to them day and night. We quoted the Word and we saw that situation nailed to the cross.

Two weeks later, on New Years Day, Tom felt like he was going to faint. Again, we had the opportunity to let the situation take us away from the blessings of God. But we still saw it nailed to the cross.

We went to the emergency room and they ran more tests. Everything came back fine. The doctor said Tom had the heart of a twenty-five-year-old. The heart condition was completely gone. In fact, it had been gone for some time. It turned out that it was the medicine that he was taking for the heart condition that made him feel like he was going to faint. Twenty years later, the doctors marvel at Tom's heart being so healthy and youthful.

The enemy wanted to distract us from a life of ministry that involved starting the church. The enemy can bite you. But you look at the cross and you live. You don't have to live with the hindrances. You can change.

## 11
## Baggage and Responsibility

A girl came to me and said that she had a great struggle in her life. She could never seem to get into the presence of God. She could pray and read the Word, but it seemed like she was unable to break through.

As we talked, she shared some things about her life and one thing that stood out was that she had been born out of wedlock. There is a verse in Deuteronomy that talks about that. It said that someone born outside of marriage was not allowed to come into the presence of God.

> *One of illegitimate birth shall not enter the assembly of the LORD, even to the tenth generation none of his descendants shall enter the assembly of the LORD.* (Deuteronomy 23:2)

This is an interesting example of a curse that is based on the law. The devil is a legalist and he delights in taking scripture and using it in a way that keeps us from God and from the blessings that are supposed to be ours. The enemy used that verse to keep this girl from experiencing the presence of God.

We prayed and asked God to forgive her mother and father and we saw that sin nailed to the cross. She was completely delivered from the effects of that sin in her parents' lives and she began to come into the presence of God and enjoy God. By the power of the cross in her life, she was completely set free. God made her legitimate and she was no longer prohibited from entering the blessing.

I mentioned the need for persistence when you are getting rid of blessing blockers in your life. If you only go half way, they will continue to cause problems for you. They must be completely eliminated.

This brings us to the fourth principle for experiencing the power of the cross. If you don't get rid of the baggage, it will be a curse to you.

God made it clear to Israel that they had to get rid of all the inhabitants of the land.

> *But if you do not drive out the inhabitants of the land from before you, then it shall be that those whom you let remain shall be irritants in your eyes and thorns in your sides, and they shall harass you in the land where you dwell.* (Numbers 33:55)

Have you ever had something in your eye and you couldn't get it out? It becomes such an irritation that all you can think about is that eye. You can't focus on anything. You can't think about anything else. It consumes your attention.

Iniquities, or generational curses, work the same way. The enemy keeps bringing them up and they take your whole attention. If you don't deal with them through the Holy Spirit, they will control your life. All of your focus is on that thing. It consumes you to the point that you never move into the promises of God.

> If you don't get rid of the baggage, it will be a curse to you.

Joshua conquered the Promised Land by getting rid of the main threats. Israel settled in the land, but there were still many of the original inhabitants there. As Joshua neared the end of his life, he told the people that they needed to persist until their enemies were completely destroyed.

> *Or else, if indeed you do go back, and cling to the remnant of these nations—these that remain among you—and make marriages with them, and go in to them and they to you, know for certain that the LORD your God will no longer drive out these nations from before you. But they shall be snares and traps to you, and scourges on your sides and thorns in your eyes, until you perish from this good land which the LORD your God has given you.* (Joshua 23:12-13)

You cannot afford to allow any of the iniquities to remain. Once the Holy Spirit reveals them to you, deal with them.

**Take Responsibility**

The fifth thing that needs to happen so that the power of the cross is released in your life is that you must take full responsibility for the iniquities that are in your life. The great men of God in the Bible confessed the iniquities of their fathers as though they had sinned themselves. We see this with Nehemiah. He prayed for God to forgive Israel.

> *Please let Your ear be attentive and Your eyes open, that You may hear the prayer of Your servant which I pray before You now, day and night, for the children of Israel Your servants, and confess the sins of the children of Israel which we have sinned against You. Both my father's house and I have sinned.* (Nehemiah 1:6)

Notice that last line. "We have sinned." Nehemiah didn't say, "Israel has sinned." He said, "We." He took personal responsibility. It was "My father's house and I" that had sinned.

The exile of Israel to Babylon came because Israel had fallen into sin and rejected God. Nehemiah wasn't there at the time. He wasn't the one who had worshipped other gods. He was a righteous man and he had not done the things his forefathers did. Yet when he prayed, he spoke as though it was his own sin.

Later, the whole nation did the same thing when they confessed the sins of their forefathers.

> *Then those of Israelite lineage separated themselves from all foreigners; and they stood and confessed their sins and the iniquities of their fathers.* (Nehemiah 9:2)

We see the same thing with Daniel. He was captured and taken to Babylon when he was very young, really just a child. He had not committed any of the sins that resulted in the destruction of Judah. Yet when he prayed about it, he spoke as though he was personally involved. He humbled himself and asked forgiveness.

> *And I prayed to the LORD my God, and made confession, and said, "O Lord, great and awesome God, who keeps His covenant and mercy with those who love Him, and with those who keep His commandments, we have sinned and committed iniquity, we have done wickedly and rebelled, even by departing from Your precepts and Your judgments.* (Daniel 9:4-5)

You have to humble yourself. The iniquities might be from your forefathers, but you need to confess them. You have to repent of them. You have to see them nailed to the cross. They are in your life until you confess them and get rid of them.

### The Power of God to Salvation

Jesus became a curse for us. His death, burial and resurrection are the power that sets us free. In fact, that is the power of the Gospel to set us free. This is what Paul had in mind when he wrote to the Romans.

> *For I am not ashamed of the gospel of Christ, for it is the power of God to salvation for everyone who believes, for the Jew first and also for the Greek.* (Romans 1:16)

The Gospel is the death, burial and resurrection. That is where the power of salvation comes from. And salvation is more than just getting to heaven. It also means being saved from the power of generational curses and saved into the abundance of God.

These five principles are steps that will unleash the power of the cross in your life. Let's review them before moving on.

1. Fellowship with the sufferings of Christ at the cross. Understand and acknowledge what He accomplished and be appreciative of it.

2. Let the Holy Spirit create the battle plan. Wait on Him to reveal what to attack next. Don't try to figure it out on your own.

3. Be willing to change. Change brings maturity and success.

4. Get rid of the baggage. Get out of denial, admit there is a problem and get rid of it.

5. Pray for the iniquities of your forefathers. Put yourself in the picture. Confess the iniquities and repent.

Turn the power of the cross loose in your life and you will see those old problems disappear. You will gain great victory and the result will be blessing and freedom from the curse.

*Damaged DNA*

# 12
## The Curse of Nationalities

A woman came to me for help one day. She had this extreme emotional behavior that would take over her emotional senses. It produced extreme inordinate desires in her. She thought that everybody thought and felt that way. But the Holy Spirit began to speak to her and tell her that it was not normal and that she needed to be free of it. It was an emotional infirmity. It wasn't a kind of behavior that she wanted. The desires that she felt were not what she wanted. Instead they violated her will.

As we talked, it became clear that she came from a nationality that is known for being very emotional. Her behavior was a result of a type of generational curse that came from her national heritage.

We began praying. We saw that curse nailed to the cross. We asked God to forgive her forefathers and her and she was instantly delivered from it. She never had that problem again. That national heritage was never able to connect to her emotions again. Her emotions became submitted to the Holy Spirit and His direction.

The effects of your national heritage are very real. As Moses prepared the people of Israel for the move into the Promised Land, he identified seven specific nations that they would encounter. He was adamant that they should completely eradicate them from the territory.

> *When the LORD your God brings you into the land which you go to possess, and has cast out many nations before you, the Hittites and the Girgashites and the Amorites and the Canaanites and the Perizzites and the Hivites and the Jebusites, seven nations greater and mightier than you, and when the LORD your God delivers them over to you, you shall conquer them and utterly destroy them. You shall make no covenant with them nor show mercy to them.* (Deuteronomy 7:1-2)

In this chapter, I want to focus specifically on those nationalities. They are a picture of the opposition that we face in entering the Promised Land that God has for us, and we need to be fully aware of what they represent. They are some of the things that God is delivering us from.

We each have a national heritage that has become so much a part of us that we tend to not think about those characteristics when we look at generational curses. But there are probably some things that you need to address that are part of your ethnic heritage. You are no longer a part of that background. You are now in the Kingdom of God, and you have a brand new DNA. You are a new nationality. You need to leave behind that past.

Abraham is a good example for us. God did not just tell him to move to a new country. He was commanded to leave behind his heritage as well.

> There are probably some things that you need to address that are part of your ethnic heritage.

*Now the LORD had said to Abram:*

*"Get out of your country.*
*From your family*
*And from your father's house,*
*To a land that I will show you.*
*I will make you a great nation;*
*I will bless you*
*And make your name great;*
*And you shall be a blessing."*

(Genesis 12:1-2)

We love to talk about the promises of blessing, but we often forget that Abraham had to leave everything behind in order to get that blessing. He had to leave his country, which is his nationality. He had to leave his family.

It is the same for us. It doesn't mean that you have to move to a foreign land. But you have to be willing to leave behind your national heritage and the character traits that go with it. You have to be willing to leave behind the family traits that are not in line with what God is doing in your life, the iniquities of your forefathers, your parents and grandparents and aunts and uncles.

We have been talking about generational curses from the perspective of family sins, but there are national sins that can affect us also. And we have to be free of them just as much as the family iniquities.

I had to deal with several things in my own life. I'm part Italian and Italians have a lot of pride. In my thirties, I had to deal with that part of my heritage. I had to get the pride out of my life.

I had a friend who had a different national heritage to deal with. She discovered that her great grandmother was married to a member of the royal family of Russia and that when the Russian Revolution broke out, her great grandfather, because of his royalty, was executed. The great grandmother, who was Swedish, escaped and hid in Sweden. When her daughter moved to America, she called herself a Norwegian so that no one would know of her Russian descent. But the Russian heritage still played a role in her life until she prayed about it and dealt with the national curse that was there.

**Paul's Heritage**

The problem is that we don't usually think of national iniquities as problems. We're usually proud of our heritage. In his letter to the Philippians, Paul talked about that very thing, and he pointed out that if anyone could boast about heritage, it was him. He had it all going for him.

> *For we are the circumcision, who worship God in the Spirit, rejoice in Christ Jesus, and have no confidence in the flesh, though I also might have confidence in the flesh. If anyone else thinks he may have confidence in the flesh, I more so: circumcised the eighth day, of the stock of Israel, of the tribe of Benjamin, a Hebrew of the Hebrews; concerning the law, a Pharisee; concerning zeal, persecuting the church; concerning the righteousness which is in the law, blameless.* (Philippians 3:3-6)

If anyone could put confidence in his heritage, Paul could. He had as good a heritage as it was possible for anyone to have. His DNA was from the stock of Israel and the tribe of Benjamin. He was the best of the best. He had religious zeal. He lived a moral life. Yet he did not put his confidence in that.

*But what things were gain to me, these I have counted loss for Christ.* (Philippians 3:7)

Paul discovered that his old DNA was of no value to him. He counted it loss. When Paul became born again, he left all of that behind. Like Abraham before him, he left his country, his family and his heritage. He realized that he had a new family now, a new father, a new household, and all of the old DNA was gone. The reason for the change was simple. He wanted to gain the blessings that are in Christ.

*Yet indeed I also count all things loss for the excellence of the knowledge of Christ Jesus my Lord, for whom I have suffered the loss of all things, and count them as rubbish, that I may gain Christ, and be found in Him, not having my own righteousness, which is from the law, but that which is through faith in Christ, the righteousness which is from God by faith.* (Philippians 3:8-9)

In other words, Paul said, "I want the knowledge of Christ Jesus. I want the anointing and the revelation of all that I am to be under my new heritage." Anything else was just rubbish.

Too many people worship their heritage. They are so proud of their ethnic background that it becomes a form of worship. They are quick to fight with anyone who doesn't give them the respect they think they deserve because of where they came from. But Paul said his heritage was loss. He had something new and better than his old nationality. He had a new bloodline that severed his ties with the old one. He was now under the blood of Jesus.

You have to be willing to let go of all the attachments of the past. Many of those national characteristics are very unhealthy. There may be certain things that are good in your national heritage, but even then, they are not things that you

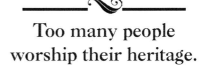

Too many people worship their heritage.

can count on any more than Paul could. That is not where your righteousness lies. It is in Christ, not in your national heritage.

You need to understand, however, that this does not mean that you completely cut off all communication with your ancestors. That is not the point. We are still to honor our father and mother.

*Children, obey your parents in the Lord, for this is right. "Honor your father and mother," which is the first commandment with promise: "that it may be well with you and you may live long on the earth."* (Ephesians 6:1-2)

We are not to neglect our parents just so we can pursue the ministry. It is the iniquities of the past that we have to deal with. We are still to love them but we must get free of the iniquities of the past. Honoring your parents is very important for your spiritual life, but it does not mean that you continue to participate in any sin or dysfunction that has been in your family in the past. As a matter of fact, you will be able to love them deeper and deeper, the more you get rid of the baggage.

> *Now that you have purified yourselves by obeying the truth so that you have sincere love for your brothers, love one another deeply, from the heart.* (1 Peter 1:22 NIV)

### The Nations of Canaan

Each of the seven nations that lived in the Promised Land had characteristics that identified them. In those national identities, we can see some of what God wants to free us from. They are really the representation of the flesh. And Paul said to put no confidence in the flesh.

The first were the Hittites. They were a fierce warrior nation who intimidated all of their neighbors. Their lives were filled with violence and anger. They represented intimidation and fear. But that is not to be a part of a believer's life. We have not been given a spirit of fear (2 Timothy 1:7).

The second nationality mentioned is the Girgashites. The name means "double-minded." Such people are controlled by unbelief. It is the kind of people that James warned about.

> *If any of you lacks wisdom, let him ask of God, who gives to all liberally and without reproach, and it will be given to him. But let him ask in faith, with no doubting, for he who doubts is like a wave of the sea driven and tossed by the wind. For let not that man suppose that he will receive anything from the Lord; he is a double-minded man, unstable in all his ways.* (James 1:5-8)

It is impossible to experience the promises of God if you are unstable and lacking faith. Double-mindedness is not of God. If that is a national curse in your life, you need to renounce it completely.

The next nation was the Amorites. Their name means "proud." They were a nation that represented a spirit of pride. They looked down on others as inferior.

Pride was the original sin. It is probably no accident that Israel encountered Amorites even before they crossed the Jordan. Sihon and Og were both Amorite kings. Pride will keep you from the blessings of God.

According to 1 Corinthians 13:4, love does not parade itself and is not puffed up. There is no room for pride in God's way of doing things. In fact, James 4:6 tells us that God resists the proud and gives grace to the humble. If you feel great pride in your nationality, you need to get rid of it.

Fourth is the Canaanites. The word Canaanite means materialism. The Canaanites had greed and selfish ambition in their lives. They took ownership of things that were not theirs and those things controlled them. They trusted in things and not in God. But, as we saw earlier, we cannot put confidence in the flesh and hope to experience the promises of God. They are not compatible.

After the Canaanites are the Perizzites. They represent a spirit of immorality. They had no boundaries or walls. There were no absolutes, no right or wrong in life. We see this spirit often in the lives of those given to addictions. They are unable to set up boundaries so they allow emotional and physical and verbal abuse to go on in their lives. They are under a curse that keeps them from putting up appropriate walls of protection.

The sixth nationality was the Hivites. The name means deceiver. They are hypocrites who live a lie. They have a spirit of compromise. They live in fear of man and consequently, they are one thing at home and something completely different in public. You never know when you are talking to the real person or just a front that they put up.

Last is the Jebusites. It is a nation that represents a spirit of depression. They live under the law of low self-esteem. They have no confidence. They are controlled by discouragement, despair and condemnation.

God said that Israel was to go into the Promised Land and drive out every one of these nationalities. You need to do the same thing. Whatever traits you have from your old DNA, your old heritage, needs to be replaced completely with your new heritage. You are now in the Kingdom of God.

In my thirties, I had to get rid of those characteristics that came from my national heritage. They were keeping me from experiencing God's best for me. From my Italian heritage, I had to get rid of pride. From the Norwegian background, there was a spirit of no walls or boundaries that had to be broken. I had to deal with that in my life.

> Whatever traits you have from your old DNA, your old heritage, needs to be replaced.

You have to let those things go or they will hinder you. They will become thorns in your eyes and prevent you from seeing the blessings of God in your life.

## 13
## Free at Last

The Promised Land is waiting for you. Jesus already provided complete victory for you so that you can live in the abundance that God intends you to have. But you have to possess the land and there are some obstacles that you have to tear down. Fortunately, through Christ we have every resource we need to do just that.

Through this book I have shared the information you need to understand what those obstacles look like and how to overcome them. Now you are ready to cross the Jordan and go into the land. You now have everything you need to break free from the blessing blockers that stand in your way. You are ready now to rid yourself of the iniquities of your forefathers.

As we close this study, I want to review just how you can be free of generational curses. The first thing that Tom and I do when we recognize a problem is we begin to fast. We usually will fast for two or three days so that we can see the Holy Spirit moving in the situation.

It is important to let the gifts of the Spirit operate. It is important to be Spirit-filled because you need all of the gifts to be working. You want to receive the word of wisdom and the word of knowledge. You want discerning of spirits and the prophetic to be operating. You need faith and healing and miracles. You need to pray in tongues and allow interpretation. It is the Holy Spirit who sets the battle plan and you need every tool that He has given to be working for you. It is important to allow the Holy Spirit to reveal things to you so that you know what step to take next.

Then, the next thing is that you have to believe. You have to be ready to admit that there's a problem and stop being in denial about it. Stop blaming everybody else and take responsibility for it. If you walk in denial, if you blame other people and make excuses, you will never change. You will keep going around and around the same mountain. You're not going to change as long as you cling to your old nationality, your old identity. You have to be ready to let it go.

Thirdly, you must recognize the importance and the power of the cross. Once you admit to the problem, then you have to receive the forgiveness of Christ. Ask God to forgive you of that sin and the sins of your forefathers. Renounce it and repent of it.

Approach it just like Daniel and Nehemiah. They were not there when Israel sinned. They didn't worship other gods, but when they prayed for God to forgive the iniquities of their fathers, they included themselves. They recognized that the power of those iniquities was at work in them, making them do things they did not want to do.

For deliverance, you then look to the cross. You see that thing nailed to the cross. When God saw Jesus hanging on the cross, he saw you and me hanging there with Him. He saw you personally. He saw every iniquity, every generational curse and every nationality curse that would ever come against you nailed there, too. He saw the price for all those sins completely paid in full.

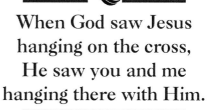

When God saw Jesus hanging on the cross, He saw you and me hanging there with Him.

We saw how the cross was foreshadowed in the Old Testament, how it pictured the crucifixion of the curse so that it would be dead and buried and no longer have any power in our lives. When Joshua defeated the kings in the Land of Promise, he hung them on a tree. Moses made a bronze serpent and put it on a pole. Deuteronomy says that anything hanging on a tree is cursed. So those incidents pictured how Jesus would later hang on a tree and become a curse for us. Through the death, burial and resurrection of Jesus, all those things that had dominion over your life were destroyed. They are now dead and buried.

Colossians 2:14-15 tells us that the requirements of the law that was against us were wiped out. Our enemies were disarmed. Every time that I have faced a problem that I couldn't overcome, we have seen it nailed to the cross and the power it had over me was broken. I triumphed over every generational curse through the power of the cross.

Knowing this, we can see that our old man, our old nature was crucified with Him. It was nailed to the cross with Jesus and the body of sin was done away with so that we are no longer slaves to sin.

Once you see yourself nailed to the cross with Jesus, then you can fellowship with His sufferings, meaning that you fellowship with Him at the cross to recognize and appreciate what He has accomplished through His death, burial and resurrection. Then you can see yourself as a coheir with Christ so that you might bring glory to Him. If we died with Christ, then we also live with Christ. We now can turn our backs on the old nature and the old way of living. We are now free from the sin. It is the blood of Jesus that makes our freedom possible.

*If we confess our sins, He is faithful and just to forgive us our sins and to cleanse us from all unrighteousness.* (1 John 1:9)

All of the unrighteousness is gone. The bloodline is clean all the way to Adam. Through the blood of Jesus, I am no longer subject to generational curses. Hebrews says that even your conscience is cleaned.

> *How much more shall the blood of Christ, who through the eternal Spirit offered Himself without spot to God, cleanse your conscience from dead works to serve the living God?* (Hebrews 9:14)

I have been brought near to God by the blood of Christ (Ephesians 2:13) and I have been completely justified by the blood (Romans 5:9).

Romans 7:4 says that I died to the law through the body of Christ and that I'm married to Him now so that I should not bear fruit to any other god. Now I can bear fruit to God in righteousness. I have been raised up with Christ to sit with Him in heavenly places. I've renounced national curses. I've renounced the iniquities of my forefathers. I've said that I won't be married to them any longer. I now belong to Jesus. I have a new DNA, a new nationality. I'm married to it one hundred percent.

I now live from blessing to blessing. I don't have a sad story to tell. I have a story of victory and success. You can have the same story. It is a simple exchange that God wants to make with you. You give up your old identity, your old nature, your old DNA, your old nationality. In return, God gives you a new nationality, new DNA, a new family. He gives you a life of abundance and freedom, freedom from sickness, freedom from poverty, freedom from every curse. Bind yourself to the promises that God has given you and don't let go. He says that if you let go of the old, He will give you new life.